ChatGPT Money Machine

Make Money Online and Level Up Your
Business With ChatGPT and the Best AI Tools

Mike Reuben

Available formats: Kindle eBook | Paperback | Hardcover | Audiobook (free with 30-day trial on Audible.com)

CONTENTS

INTRODUCTION

In today's rapidly evolving digital landscape, the potential to generate income online has never been more accessible. As artificial intelligence (AI) continues to advance at a breakneck pace, many opportunities have emerged for those savvy enough to harness its potential. *ChatGPT Money Machine* is your comprehensive guide to unlocking the secrets of this growing field, providing you with the tools and knowledge you need to create your online business empire.

This book will lead you on a journey through the world of AI-driven online revenue generation, offering insights and practical advice that will help you tap into the vast potential of AI-powered platforms like ChatGPT. You will learn how to leverage these cutting-edge technologies to develop innovative business ideas, streamline your operations, and maximize your profits.

As you delve into this captivating exploration of the AI frontier, you'll discover how to capitalize on the strengths of ChatGPT and similar tools to create engaging content, build a loyal customer base, and stay ahead of the competition in the ever-evolving online marketplace. In addition, we'll examine various business ventures, ideas, and opportunities, providing you with the inspiration and motivation you need to forge your path to online success.

Whether you're a seasoned entrepreneur looking to expand your digital presence, a curious newcomer eager to embrace the AI revolution, or a tech enthusiast seeking to turn your passion into profit, *ChatGPT Money Machine* will equip you with the knowledge and tools to make your dreams a reality. So welcome to the forefront of the AI-driven online income revolution—your journey to success begins here.

Let's enjoy the ride together.

Regards,

Mike Reuben

1. WHAT IS AI?

Artificial intelligence (AI) is computer software that mimics human cognitive abilities to perform complex tasks that historically could only be done by humans, such as decision-making, data analysis, and language translation.

AI has wide-ranging capabilities and implications that produce various impactful real-world applications. AI capabilities include pattern recognition, predictive modeling, automation, object recognition, and personalization; for instance, self-driving cars and chatbots use AI.

AI-powered machines and systems can learn from their interactions to improve their performance and efficiency. Also, AI code is used to perform tasks that require human reasoning. By contrast, automated machines and systems follow a set of instructions and execute them without change or self-improvement.

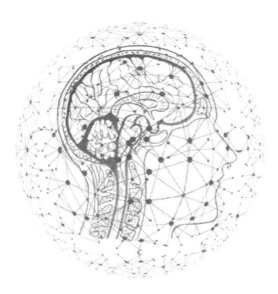

Image credit: Gerd Altmann from Pixabay

The World of AI

AI is a catchall term covering a variety of interrelated but distinct subfields. Some of the most common fields include the following:

Machine learning (ML) is a subset of AI in which algorithms are trained on data sets to become machine learning models capable of performing specific tasks.

Deep learning is a subset of ML in which artificial neural networks (AANs) that mimic the human brain are used to perform more complex reasoning tasks without human intervention.

Natural Language Processing (NLP) is a subset of computer science, AI, linguistics, and ML focused on creating software capable of interpreting human communication.

Robotics is a subset of AI, computer science, and electrical engineering focused on creating robots capable of learning and performing complex tasks in real-world environments.

Coursera, an e-learning company, has a course about AI called "AI for Everyone." So, if you want to become more familiar with AI, it's an excellent class to take for techies and non-techies alike.

AI Has Been Here for Awhile

ChatGPT is a giant leap forward in AI, exciting millions of people, organizations, and businesses globally. However, individuals and businesses have been using AI for decades.

The use of AI in business can be traced back to the 1950s and 1960s, when the concept of artificial intelligence began to emerge. However, early AI applications were limited in scope and practicality due to technological limitations and high costs.

In the 1980s, businesses started to adopt AI more widely, mainly in the form of expert systems. These were rule-based systems designed to mimic human decision-making in specific domains, such as medical diagnosis, financial planning, and manufacturing. Expert systems were among the first practical applications of AI in businesses.

The 1990s saw the development of machine learning algorithms, which allowed computers to learn from data without explicit programming. This led to the growth of AI applications in areas like data mining, fraud detection, and customer relationship management (CRM).

In the 2000s, with the increasing availability of big data, improvements in computing power, and advances in AI algorithms, businesses started to adopt AI on a much larger scale. Applications expanded to include natural language processing, computer vision, and recommender systems.

Today, AI has become integral to many businesses across various industries, including healthcare, finance, retail, manufacturing, transportation, and more. AI technologies such as machine learning, deep learning, and neural networks are used to automate processes, analyze data, and provide actionable insights, enabling businesses to become more efficient and competitive.

Everyday AI

AI is increasingly integrated into our daily lives without many of us noticing. Here are some everyday examples of AI:

Virtual Assistants: Siri, Alexa, Google Assistant, and Cortana are AI-powered voice-activated assistants that help users perform tasks, answer questions, and control smart home devices.

Social Media Algorithms: Facebook, Instagram, TikTok, and Twitter use AI algorithms to personalize content, suggest friends, and filter out spam or harmful content.

Email Filters: AI-driven spam filters in Gmail, Outlook, and other email services learn from users' behavior to separate spam and phishing emails from genuine ones.

Online Advertising: AI is used to personalize and optimize online ads, targeting users based on their browsing habits and interests.

Recommender Systems: Platforms like Netflix, YouTube, and Spotify use AI algorithms to analyze user preferences and suggest content tailored to their tastes.

Chatbots and Virtual Support: AI-powered chatbots provide customer support, answer queries, and assist with bookings on websites and apps.

Smart Home Devices: AI-driven devices like Nest thermostats, Ring doorbells, and Roomba robotic vacuum cleaners learn from users' habits to automate and optimize various tasks.

Navigation and Traffic: AI-powered apps like Google Maps and Waze analyze traffic patterns and offer optimized routes in real time.

Language Translation: AI-based tools like Google Translate and DeepL enable real-time text and speech translation across multiple languages.

Autocorrect and Predictive Text: AI algorithms in smartphones and other devices help with spelling and grammar corrections and predict the next word in a sentence.

Face Recognition: Smartphone unlock features, photo tagging on social media, and security systems use AI-based face recognition technology.

Those examples represent a fraction of the AI applications in use today, and AI technology continues to evolve rapidly globally.

2. CHATGPT EXPLAINED

ChatGPT is an AI language model developed by OpenAI based on the GPT (Generative Pre-trained Transformer) architecture. It is designed to generate human-like text responses in a conversational setting. The primary function of ChatGPT is to assist users by answering questions, providing suggestions, and engaging in coherent and context-aware conversations.

The underlying technology of ChatGPT is a transformer architecture, a type of deep learning model that excels in handling sequential data, such as text. The model is pre-trained on a large body of text from the internet, allowing it to learn grammar, facts, reasoning abilities, and some level of common sense. However, it's important to note that its knowledge is limited to the training data and may not always be current or accurate.

The model works by using a technique called "self-attention" to weigh and analyze the relationships between words in each context. It can generate context-aware responses by predicting the most likely next word in a sequence, given the previous terms.

To fine-tune ChatGPT for specific tasks or domains, it is trained on custom datasets, often involving human-generated dialogues. This process helps the model understand the nuances of conversation and improves its ability to generate relevant and coherent responses.

While ChatGPT is a powerful AI language model, it may still produce incorrect or nonsensical answers. However, the technology continues to evolve, and improvements are being made to enhance its capabilities and reduce potential biases in its responses.

Introducing ChatGPT

We've trained a model called ChatGPT which interacts in a conversational way. The dialogue format makes it possible for ChatGPT to answer followup questions, admit its mistakes, challenge incorrect premises, and reject inappropriate requests.

Image credit: OpenAI

Benefits and Drawbacks

Arguably, "smart money" investors believe ChatGPT's benefits far outweigh its drawbacks, which is why Microsoft and other prominent investors have poured billions into OpenAI.

To mitigate the drawbacks and maximize the benefits of ChatGPT, it is essential to use it as a complementary tool alongside human expertise and judgment, ensuring that its responses are accurate, appropriate, and contextually relevant.

The benefits of using ChatGPT include the following:

Speed and efficiency: ChatGPT can provide instant responses, making it useful for tasks that require quick information retrieval or assistance, such as customer support, content generation, or answering questions.

Availability: ChatGPT can operate 24/7, making it a valuable resource for users across different time zones and schedules.

Scalability: AI-powered chatbots like ChatGPT can handle multiple simultaneous conversations, allowing businesses to scale their customer support and engagement efforts without significant increases in human resources.

Language proficiency: ChatGPT has a firm grasp of grammar, syntax, and context, making it practical for tasks involving natural language understanding and generation.

Cost-effectiveness: In the long run, ChatGPT can reduce labor costs associated with tasks like customer service, content creation, and data analysis. Also, ChatGPT offers free and paid plans.

Personalization: ChatGPT can be fine-tuned for specific domains, industries, or tasks, allowing for tailored user experiences and more relevant responses.

The drawbacks of using ChatGPT include the following:

Limited understanding: ChatGPT may sometimes provide incorrect or nonsensical answers due to its reliance on training data and lack of real-world experience.

Lack of empathy and emotions: As an AI model, ChatGPT cannot genuinely empathize with users, which may make its responses less appropriate or satisfactory in certain situations.

Incomplete or outdated knowledge: ChatGPT's ability is limited to its training data and may not include the latest information, trends, or events.

Bias: AI models like ChatGPT can inadvertently learn and reproduce biases present in their training data, leading to biased or inappropriate responses.

Over-dependency: Relying too much on ChatGPT for decision-making or critical tasks can be risky, as it may not always provide accurate or contextually appropriate responses.

Privacy and security: AI-driven chatbots raise concerns about user data privacy, as conversations may contain sensitive information that could be exposed or misused. For example, Italy was the first Western country to ban ChatGPT for privacy concerns.

Legal Implications

I can imagine countless lawyers salivating at the prospects of legal fees concerning ChatGPT and other AI chatbots because lawsuits frequently piggyback new technologies. For example, Big Tech companies like Apple, Microsoft, and Alphabet have spent millions to billions on lawyers and lawsuits globally.

As AI technology and its applications continue to evolve, the legal landscape will likely develop parallel to address the unique challenges posed by AI-driven systems like ChatGPT and other chatbots.

ChatGPT and other AI chatbots have several legal implications that businesses and users should be aware of. Some of the critical areas of concern include:

Data privacy and protection: AI chatbots often process personal data, which raises concerns about user privacy. Compliance with data protection regulations like GDPR, CCPA, and other regional privacy laws is crucial to protect user information and avoid potential legal consequences.

Intellectual property: The content generated by AI chatbots may raise questions about copyright ownership, mainly if the output is used for commercial purposes. Determining whether the AI model, its developers, or users own the rights to the generated content is an ongoing legal debate.

Liability and accountability: Determining responsibility in cases where AI chatbots cause harm, provide incorrect information, or make decisions that lead to financial or reputational loss can be challenging. The lack of a clear legal framework for AI accountability makes assigning liability in such situations difficult.

Transparency and disclosure: Users should be made aware when interacting with an AI chatbot rather than a human. Regulations like California's B.O.T. Act require companies to disclose the use of automated chatbots in specific contexts, ensuring transparency and informed consent.

Bias and discrimination: AI models, including chatbots, can perpetuate biases present in their training data, which may lead to unfair treatment of certain groups. Compliance with anti-discrimination laws is essential to avoid legal ramifications and maintain an inclusive user experience.

Security: Ensuring that AI chatbots are designed and deployed securely is critical to protect user data and prevent unauthorized access or misuse. Legal obligations regarding safeguarding user information and maintaining secure systems should be followed.

To address these legal implications, businesses should:

- Ensure compliance with data protection and privacy regulations locally and abroad.
- Be transparent about their use of AI chatbots and provide appropriate disclosures.
- Continuously monitor and audit chatbot performance to identify and rectify biases, inaccuracies, or security vulnerabilities.
- Consult legal experts to understand the evolving legal landscape surrounding AI and chatbots and develop strategies to manage potential risks and liabilities.

First, ChatGPT and other AI tools aren't magic wands or genies. Instead, AI tools are only as good as the user's input and skills. That's what differentiates one user from the next. Secondly, many AI apps offer free and paid plans, the latter providing more features. So, getting optimal results may depend on the method chosen.

Prompt Mastery

A prompt is the starting point of a conversation in the form of a question or instruction given to an AI language model like ChatGPT.

Using the same prompts as everyone else could result in undifferentiated responses and outcomes. That won't benefit you when making money online because you'll lack differentiation and uniqueness. So, consider how you can tweak common prompts to develop unique questions and instructions.

To get the best results from ChatGPT, users can follow these tips:

- Start with an action word or request: use a verb to instruct a chatbot what to do, for example, write, create, recommend, etc. Be specific: Clearly define your question or request, and provide enough context to help the AI understand the desired outcome. Vague or ambiguous prompts may result in unclear or irrelevant responses.
- Specify the format: If you have a specific format in mind for the response (e.g., a list, a paragraph, or step-by-step instructions), mention it in your prompt to guide the AI in generating an appropriate answer.
- Ask for pros, cons, or comparisons: If you're looking for a balanced perspective or comparing different options, explicitly request pros, cons, or a comparison in your prompt.
- Include relevant context: If your question or request refers to a particular situation, event, or time, provide enough background information to help the AI generate a relevant and accurate response.
- Set a word limit: If you need a response with a specific word count, indicate the desired length in your prompt. For example, you could ask for a "brief summary" or a "detailed explanation" depending on your requirements.
- Use step-by-step or follow-up questions: If your topic is complex, consider breaking it down into smaller parts or asking follow-up questions to clarify or expand on the initial response.
- Proofread and refine: If the AI's response isn't what you expected or needs improvement, try rephrasing your prompt or providing additional context. Experimenting with different ways to frame your question can help you obtain better results.

- Keep it simple: While ChatGPT can understand complex questions, it's best to keep your questions simple and easy to understand. This will help ensure that you get the most accurate and relevant responses.
- Give examples: reference an example or examples to assist ChatGPT with what you want to achieve.
- Provide feedback: If ChatGPT's response is not helpful or doesn't answer your question, let it know by providing feedback. This helps it learn and improve its responses over time.

Google "best chatgpt prompts" or "best chatbot prompts" with your profession or interest to find listicles of prompts, for example, "best chatgpt prompts for marketers." Also, read "How to Write the Perfect ChatGPT Prompt and Become a ChatGPT Expert" by Writesonic, and visit awesomegptprompts.com for more insights.

Prompt: "Give me 15 hashtags for a YouTube video about passive income"

1. #PassiveIncomeIdeas
2. #IncomeStreams
3. #FinancialFreedom
4. #MoneyGoals
5. #SmartInvesting
6. #ResidualIncome
7. #WealthBuilding
8. #SideHustleSuccess
9. #AutomatedIncome
10. #EarnWhileYouSleep
11. #OnlineBusiness
12. #PassiveProfits
13. #InvestmentStrategies
14. #CashFlowGrowth
15. #FinancialIndependence

Image credit: OpenAI

ChatGPT Alternatives

Welcome to the new Bing

Your AI-powered copilot for the web

 Get better answers

Image credit: Bing

Things got very interesting after the release of ChatGPT in November 2022. For example, the cofounders of Google (Alphabet), Larry Page and Sergey Brin, held an emergency meeting to discuss ChatGPT and its potential impact on search, according to The New York Times. Then, Alphabet quickly launched "Bard" to compete with ChatGPT. However, Bard received a lukewarm public response because of its disappointing and questionable responses.

There are several ChatGPT chatbot alternatives that users can explore. Here are some of the most popular ones:

Bing AI is a set of artificial intelligence technologies and services developed by Microsoft for their search engine, Bing. These AI technologies and services are designed to enhance the user experience and improve the accuracy and relevance of search results. Bing AI uses OpenAI's most advanced LLM, GPT-4.

Microsoft Bot Framework is a platform that enables developers to build intelligent bots that can interact with users across various platforms like Skype, Facebook Messenger, and Slack.

Google Bard is an AI language model developed by Google that aims to improve the ability of machines to understand and generate poetry. It is named after the famous English poet William Shakespeare, one of the greatest poets ever.

Dialogflow is a natural language processing platform developed by Google that allows developers to build conversational interfaces for websites, mobile applications, and messaging platforms.

IBM Watson Assistant is a chatbot development platform that uses natural language processing and machine learning to understand and respond to user requests in real time.

Amazon Lex is a service for building conversational interfaces into voice and text applications.

Ras is an open-source chatbot development framework that enables developers to create chatbots with customized natural language understanding and machine learning models.

Botpress is an open-source chatbot development platform that allows developers to create and deploy custom chatbots with advanced natural language understanding capabilities.

3. MAKE MONEY ONLINE WITH CHATGPT & AI TOOLS

Millions of individuals have been making money online since the early 2000s. The adoption and emerging technologies of the internet allow people to earn passive and active income, start businesses quickly, pivot instantly, advertise and sell globally, be their own bosses, work from anywhere, and gain independence.

Getting Started and Monetization

Making money online begins with understanding the platforms and apps you can use to run a business. For example, in e-commerce, you can start an online store and sell physical or digital products through platforms like Shopify, WooCommerce, Amazon, and Etsy. Shopify and WooCommerce support independent retail websites, whereas Amazon and Etsy offer online marketplaces comprising millions of sellers.

In the content creation category, you can create and share content on platforms like YouTube, Instagram, and TikTok. Then, you can monetize your content through sponsorships, ad revenue, affiliate marketing, and selling products.

We'll dive deeper into getting started and monetization for various online endeavors.

ChatGPT, Prompt Examples, and AI Tools

By bringing AI tools into the mix, digital entrepreneurs and businesses can save time, increase efficiency and productivity, and make more informed decisions with data-driven insights. Some benefits of AI tools include optimization, personalization, predictive analysis, and automation. For example, AI tools can automate repetitive or mundane tasks, freeing time and resources for more complex or creative work.

You or AI Tools?

Sometimes, ChatGPT and other AI tools can do most or all the work for you. For example, you can rely heavily on AI tools for the written component of blogging. In other cases, however, you'll do most of the work and use AI tools to increase productivity, save time, improve workflows, optimize results, and make better decisions.

Creativity, originality, and risk-taking are the root of most successful creators, freelancers, sellers, entrepreneurs, and developers. So, if you heavily depend on AI tools to generate income and don't contribute enough of your unique capabilities, you might end up disappointed with the results. Furthermore, you may disappoint the people and businesses that trust you to deliver excellent work. So, it's critical to strike a balance between AI use and your skills to rise above your competitors and achieve your goals.

Let's begin your online income journey with content creation.

Discover my favorite online business and marketing apps: https://subscribepage.io/mike-reuben

4. MAKE MONEY ONLINE WITH CONTENT

From YouTube to your favorite blog and online courses to a book you're reading, content is everywhere, and the category constantly expands and evolves. So, for example, content has room to flourish in the metaverse.

Content creation refers to creating content, such as written articles, videos, podcasts, social media posts, and images. The purpose of content creation is to produce informative, entertaining, or educational material that engages and interests the intended audience.

The content creation process typically involves several steps, including researching the topic, planning the content, creating the material, and publishing or distributing it. However, the exact steps involved in content creation can vary depending on the type of content being made, as well as the purpose and goals of the content.

Effective content creation requires a combination of creativity, research skills, and technical expertise, depending on the type of content being produced. For example, a blog post may require strong writing skills and an understanding of search engine optimization (SEO), while a video may require skills in videography, editing, and graphic design.

YouTubers

Each year, multiple media outlets list the highest-paid YouTubers. Their annual revenues resemble those of top-performing professional athletes and A-list celebrities. So, it's no wonder YouTube is one of the most exciting opportunities for those aspiring to make money online.

A YouTuber creates and publishes video content on YouTube. They typically produce various videos, from educational and informational content to entertainment and lifestyle content. Successful YouTubers are those who can consistently create engaging and high-quality content and build a loyal and engaged fan base.

Getting Started

First, a YouTube creator requires creativity, dedication, and a willingness to learn and adapt. Secondly, becoming a YouTube creator involves several steps, including the following:

1. Create a YouTube account: If you don't already have a YouTube account, sign up for one. You can use an existing Google account to sign in or create a new account specifically for YouTube.
2. Plan your content: Decide what type of videos you want to create and plan your content accordingly. Consider your interests and passions and what you want to share with your audience.
3. Invest in equipment: Depending on the type of videos you want to create, you may need to invest in equipment like a camera, microphone, and lighting.
4. Start creating and uploading videos: Once you have your content planned and your equipment ready, start creating and uploading videos to your YouTube channel. Aim to create high-quality content that is engaging and informative.

5. Optimize your videos: To ensure that your videos are discoverable by your target audience, optimize your videos with relevant keywords, titles, and descriptions.
6. Promote your channel: Promote your channel on social media, your website, and other relevant platforms to attract new subscribers and viewers.
7. Engage with your audience: Respond to comments, create a community around your channel, and collaborate with other YouTubers to build engagement and loyalty.

Monetization

YouTube Partner Program Eligibility

Image credit: Google

YouTubers can make money through a combination of advertising revenue, sponsorships, merchandise sales, crowdfunding, affiliate marketing, and fan support. The amount of money earned can vary widely depending on factors such as the YouTuber's niche, audience size, and content quality.

Advertising revenue—YouTube displays ads before, during, and after videos, and YouTubers can earn a portion of the ad revenue generated from their videos. The amount of money made depends on factors such as the number of views, the length of the video, and the advertiser's budget.

Sponsorships—YouTubers can earn money by partnering with brands and promoting their products or services in their videos. In exchange, the YouTuber may receive a fee or free products.

Merchandise sales—Many YouTubers sell merchandise, such as t-shirts, mugs, and phone cases, featuring their logo or catchphrase. The YouTuber may receive a percentage of the sales revenue.

Affiliate marketing—YouTubers can earn a commission by promoting products or services in their videos and including affiliate links in the video description.

Fan support—Some viewers may donate money to their favorite YouTubers directly through platforms like YouTube Super Chat, which allows viewers to pay to have their messages highlighted during live streams.

Using ChatGPT

ChatGPT can help YouTubers in several ways, such as the following examples:

Content ideas: ChatGPT can provide ideas for new video content based on a YouTuber's niche, audience, and interests. YouTubers can ask ChatGPT open-ended questions about their channel and get suggestions for new topics to cover.

Video optimization: ChatGPT can help optimize videos by suggesting video titles, tags, descriptions, and other metadata. YouTubers can ask ChatGPT questions about how to optimize their videos for search engines and get helpful suggestions.

Collaboration opportunities: ChatGPT can help with collaboration opportunities by suggesting other YouTubers or influencers to collaborate with based on a YouTuber's niche and audience.

Scriptwriting: ChatGPT can help with scriptwriting by providing suggestions for video scripts or voiceovers.

YouTubers can ask ChatGPT questions about structuring their videos and getting ideas for engaging content.

Channel growth strategies: ChatGPT can provide suggestions for channel growth strategies based on a YouTuber's niche and audience. YouTubers can ask ChatGPT questions about increasing their subscribers, views, and engagement and get ideas for effective growth strategies.

Prompt Examples

- "Generate eight unique video ideas for a travel-focused YouTube channel."
- "Write an engaging intro script for a YouTube video reviewing the latest mirrorless camera."
- "Suggest seven attention-grabbing video titles for a vlog about a day in the life of a remote worker."
- "What text should I include on a thumbnail for a video about budget beauty tips?"
- "Write a compelling YouTube description for a channel about vegan cooking, health, and lifestyle."
- "List 10 relevant video tags for a YouTube guide on how to edit videos using Adobe Premiere Pro."

AI Tools for YouTubers

Descript is an AI-based editing software that enables users to edit video and audio files by editing the text transcript. It also provides automatic transcription, translation, and voice-over features.

Headliner.app is an AI-based online video editor that enables YouTubers to create audiograms, subtitles, and social media video promos.

Wavve.co is an AI-powered tool that helps YouTubers create custom video clips and audiograms for social media promotion.

InVideo is an AI-powered video editing platform that allows YouTubers to create, edit, and customize videos using templates, automated voice-overs, and advanced editing tools.

Music Generation: AI-driven tools like Jukedeck and AIVA can compose original background music tailored to the mood and style of a video.

Spotlight: TubeBuddy

Tube Buddy   PRICING   ENTERPRISE

Optimize your
YouTube channel
FASTER

Image credit: TubeBuddy

TubeBuddy is a browser extension and mobile app designed to help YouTube content creators streamline their workflow and optimize their videos for better performance on the platform.

TubeBuddy is available in free and paid versions, with premium features available through various pricing plans, including Pro, Star, Legend, and Enterprise.

TubeBuddy offers a wide range of tools and features that assist YouTubers with various aspects of channel management and growth, such as:

Keyword research: TubeBuddy provides keyword suggestions and analysis to help creators choose the best keywords, tags, and titles for their videos, improving search rankings and visibility.

SEO optimization: The tool offers a checklist of best practices and optimization strategies to ensure that videos are optimized for YouTube's search algorithm.

Thumbnail generation: TubeBuddy's built-in thumbnail creator allows users to design custom, eye-catching thumbnails for their videos.

Bulk processing: Creators can make changes to multiple videos at once, such as updating descriptions, adding annotations, or modifying end screens, saving time and effort.

Competitor analysis: TubeBuddy allows users to monitor competitor channels and compare their performance to identify growth opportunities and strategies.

Video analytics: The tool provides detailed insights on video performance, such as audience demographics, watch time, and traffic sources, helping creators make data-driven decisions for future content.

Promotion and sharing: TubeBuddy offers tools to help promote videos on social media platforms and online communities, driving traffic and increasing viewer engagement.

Comment management: Creators can filter, sort, and manage comments more efficiently using TubeBuddy's comment moderation tools.

Integration with other tools: TubeBuddy can be integrated with other popular tools and services, such as Google Analytics, Canva, and Trello, for a more seamless content creation experience.

AI Tools

AI Title Generator—The TubeBuddy AI title generator harnesses the power of NLP to help YouTubers improve results. After you input your initial title idea or keywords, the tool will generate several more. You can use one of these titles, take inspiration from them, or even use them to run A/B tests.

31

A/B Testing—TubeBuddy allows users to test different video elements, such as titles, descriptions, and thumbnails, to determine which variations perform best.

Spotlight: VidIQ

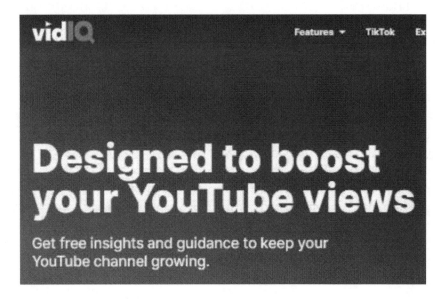

Image credit: VidIQ

VidIQ is a browser extension and web app designed to help YouTube content creators optimize their videos, grow their channels, and improve their overall performance on the platform.

VidIQ has free and paid versions, with premium features accessible through various pricing plans, including Pro, Boost, and Max.

VidIQ offers a range of tools and features that assist creators in various aspects of YouTube channel management, including:

Keyword research: VidIQ provides keyword suggestions, search volume data, and competition analysis to help creators choose the most effective keywords, tags, and titles for their videos, improving search rankings and visibility.

SEO optimization: The tool offers an optimization checklist and scores videos based on their metadata, helping creators ensure their videos are optimized for YouTube's search algorithm.

Video analytics: VidIQ provides detailed insights into video performance, audience demographics, watch time, engagement metrics, and more, enabling creators to make data-driven decisions for future content.

Competitor analysis: VidIQ allows users to track competitor channels, compare their performance, and identify growth opportunities and strategies.

Trend alerts: Creators can receive notifications about trending topics and popular keywords, allowing them to capitalize on emerging trends and create relevant content.

Best time to post: VidIQ analyzes viewer engagement patterns to recommend the best times for creators to upload new videos, maximizing views and audience engagement.

Channel audit: The tool provides an overview of a channel's performance, highlighting areas for improvement and suggesting actionable recommendations for growth.

Comment management: VidIQ offers tools to filter, sort, and manage comments more efficiently, helping creators engage with their audience and maintain a positive community.

Video promotion: VidIQ helps creators share their content on various social media platforms, online communities, and websites to drive traffic and increase visibility.

Integration with other platforms: VidIQ can be integrated with other popular tools and services, such as Google Analytics, for a more seamless content creation experience.

AI Tools

Daily Ideas—A machine learning model that generates content ideas by analyzing other channels that produce similar content to yours and your videos.

Titles and descriptions—Type in a keyword or title for recommendations after the video upload.

AI Coach—A tool using GPT-3 to support your creative journey and questions.

Influencers

How would you like to get paid thousands for each of your social media posts? Consequently, many influencers experience that globally.

An influencer has the power to "influence" the purchasing decisions, opinions, or behaviors of others due to their authority, knowledge, position, or relationship with their audience. Influencers typically have a large and engaged following on social media platforms like Instagram, YouTube, Twitter, TikTok, or personal blogs. They can be from various backgrounds, such as celebrities, industry experts, content creators, or people who have gained a significant online presence.

Influencers often collaborate with brands to promote products or services to their audience through sponsored content, reviews, or endorsements. Their influence on their followers makes them valuable marketing partners for businesses seeking to reach specific target audiences or create brand awareness. As a result, influencer marketing has become an increasingly popular and effective strategy in the digital age.

Influencer earnings mainly depend on the number of followers they have. You can use these guidelines to start.

- Nano-influencer: 1,000–10,000 followers ($10–$100 per post)
- Micro-influencer: 10,000–50,000 followers ($100–$500 per post)
- Mid-tier influencer: 50,000–500,000 followers ($500–$5,000 per post)
- Macro-influencer: 500,000–1 million followers ($5,000–$10,000 per post)
- Mega-influencer: 1 million+ followers ($10,000–$1 million+ per post)

Instagram

elvis ✅   Follow

2,013 posts   1.7M

Elvis Presley
Official page for the King
elvis.warnerbros.com

Followed by **muhammadali**

Image credit: Instagram

An Instagrammer, sometimes referred to as an Instagram influencer or content creator, uses the social media platform Instagram to share visual content, such as photos, videos, and Stories. They typically have many followers and engage with their audience through likes, comments, and direct messages. Instagrammers can focus on various niches, such as fashion, travel, fitness, lifestyle, food, or photography, among others. Their activities and objectives can include the following:

Creating content: Instagrammers produce high-quality, visually appealing content that caters to their target audience's interests and preferences. This content can include images, videos, Reels, and Stories.

Growing their audience: They work on attracting and retaining followers through regular content updates, engaging captions, and consistent posting schedules. Instagrammers may also use hashtags, location tags, and collaborations with other influencers to expand their reach.

Engaging with followers: Instagrammers interact with their audience through comments, likes, and direct messages, fostering a sense of community and building a loyal fan base.

Collaborating with brands: Many Instagrammers collaborate with brands to create sponsored content, promoting products or services to their audience in exchange for compensation or free products. They may also use affiliate marketing to earn commissions from their recommended products.

Building their brand: Instagrammers often work on establishing themselves as experts or authorities in their chosen niche, which can lead to business opportunities, partnerships, or even traditional media exposure.

Networking: Instagrammers may attend events, conferences, or workshops to connect with fellow content creators, brands, and industry professionals, enabling them to learn, grow and collaborate.

TikTok

A TikToker creates videos on the social media platform TikTok. TikTok is a platform where users can create and share short-form videos, typically 15 to 60 seconds long, set to music or other audio. TikTok videos often feature creative and entertaining content, such as dances, lip-syncing, comedy skits, and challenges.

TikTokers create content on the platform by recording and editing videos using the TikTok app. They can use various features, including filters, effects, and music libraries, to enhance their videos and make them more engaging. TikTokers often aim to create entertaining, informative, or relatable content for their audiences.

TikTokers can also engage with their audience by responding to comments, participating in challenges, and collaborating with other creators. In addition, they may use hashtags to help their content get discovered by a wider audience.

Some TikTokers may use the platform to build their brand or promote their business. They may work with brands or other creators on sponsored content, use TikTok to drive traffic to their website or other social media channels or use TikTok to showcase their skills or talents.

Getting Started

Getting started on Instagram or TikTok involve creating an account, exploring the app, creating your first post, and engaging with the community. Then, you can build a following and grow your presence on the platform by consistently posting engaging content and engaging with other users.

Monetization

Instagrammers and TikTokers can earn money through brand partnerships, sponsored posts, merchandise sales, ad revenue, and affiliate marketing. Additionally, TikTokers can make money with the following:

Live streaming: TikTokers can earn money by live streaming on the platform. Fans can send virtual gifts to TikTokers during live streams, and TikTokers can convert these gifts into real money.

Creator Fund: TikTok has a Creator Fund that pays eligible TikTokers to create engaging content on the platform. The fund is based on views, engagement, and other factors.

Using ChatGPT

Content creation: ChatGPT can generate high-quality, creative, and engaging content tailored to an influencer's niche and audience. This can include generating captions, blog posts, video scripts, and even brainstorming ideas for new content formats, enabling influencers to maintain a steady stream of fresh content and keep their audience engaged.

Audience interaction: Engaging with followers is crucial for influencers to build and maintain a loyal community. ChatGPT can help influencers craft personalized and well-thought-out responses to comments and messages, ensuring their audience feels valued and heard.

Social media strategy: Influencers can use ChatGPT to generate insights and ideas for an effective social media strategy. It can help plan content schedules, identify trending topics, and suggest potential collaboration partners.

Brand collaborations: ChatGPT can assist influencers in creating persuasive pitches for brand collaborations and sponsorships. It can also generate content that adheres to brand guidelines and messaging while maintaining the influencer's authentic voice, making sponsored content more appealing to both brands and followers.

Time-saving: By streamlining various aspects of content creation and audience engagement, ChatGPT saves influencers valuable time, enabling them to focus on other aspects of their career, such as personal branding, networking, and business development.

Analyzing performance: ChatGPT can be used to analyze the performance of influencers' content, identifying patterns and trends that can help them optimize their strategy for maximum engagement and growth.

Hashtag suggestions: ChatGPT can offer relevant hashtags to use in posts.

Prompt Examples

- "What are your favorite fashion and beauty trends of the season? Share your top picks and how to style them."
- "What are your go-to healthy recipes for busy weekends? Give instructions on how you prepare them and share your favorite ingredients."
- "How do you maintain a healthy work-life balance while managing your online presence? Share your tips, recommendations, and advice."
- "What are your top 5 must-have cosmetic products? Share a tutorial on how you use them to create your unique look."
- "Share a before-and-after story, whether it's related to fitness, fashion, self-development, travel, or home organization."

AI Tools for Instagrammers

Image credit: Hootsuite

Hootsuite Insights is an AI-powered social media monitoring tool that can help Instagrammers track their engagement, analyze their followers, and identify trends and opportunities.

Later.com is an AI-powered Instagram scheduling and analytics tool that can help Instagrammers plan and optimize their content. It includes a visual content calendar, post preview, and hashtag suggestions.

Influencer.co is an AI-powered influencer marketing platform that can help Instagrammers find brand collaborations and sponsorship opportunities based on their audience and engagement metrics.

Combin.com is an AI-powered Instagram growth tool that can help Instagrammers increase their followers, engagement, and reach. It includes features like automated likes, comments, and follow/unfollow actions.

SocialFox is an AI-powered Instagram management tool that can help Instagrammers analyze their followers, track their engagement, and optimize their content. It includes features like audience segmentation, scheduling, and hashtag analysis.

AI Tools for TikTokers

ByteDance is the parent company of TikTok, and it offers a suite of creator tools that can help users improve their videos. These tools include features like video effects, music libraries, and analytics.

TrendTok is an AI-powered application that lets users discover the latest trends on TikTok. It's useful as a tool to supplement TikTok's Discover tab to identify what's trending.

HypeAuditor is an AI-powered influencer marketing platform that can help TikTokers grow their audience. It can analyze users' followers and provide insights into their demographics and interests.

InShot is a video editing tool that can help TikTokers create high-quality videos. It offers features like trimming, cropping, and adding music to videos.

Lumen5 is an AI-powered video creation platform that can help TikTokers turn blog posts, articles, or text-based content into engaging videos.

Nova A.I. is designed for you to make video editing for TikTok straightforward. Cut, Trim, merge, and resize your videos with just a single click of a button.

Bloggers

Blogging is one of the OGs of making money online, with many bloggers starting in the mid-2000s. It was simple to begin by purchasing web hosting services and using a content management system (CMS) like WordPress. Next thing you knew, you were publishing content for the world to find and read.

Bloggers create, publish, and manage content on a blog. Their activities typically include a variety of tasks related to content creation, promotion, and community engagement.

Blogging can serve various purposes, such as:

- Personal expression: Many bloggers use their blogs to share their thoughts, opinions, and personal experiences on topics they are passionate about or interested in.
- Education and information: Bloggers can create content to educate or inform readers about a specific subject, provide tutorials or guides, or share the latest news and trends.
- Business promotion: Companies and entrepreneurs often use blogs to promote their products or services, share industry insights, and build relationships with their customers or clients.
- Networking and community building: Blogging allows individuals to connect with others who share similar interests or goals, fostering a sense of community and encouraging collaboration.

Getting Started

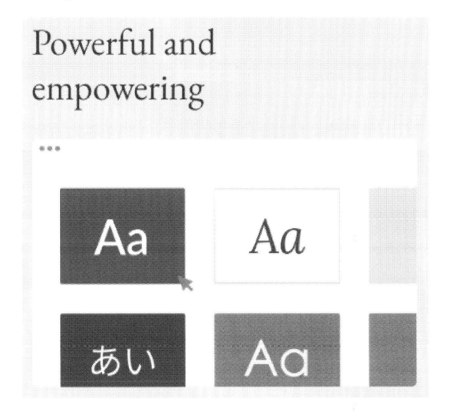

Image credit: WordPress

A person needs to choose a blogging platform (such as WordPress, Blogger, or Medium), select a domain name, set up web hosting (if using a self-hosted platform), and design the blog's layout and appearance.

Once the blog is set up, a blogger can create and publish content regularly to engage his readers and grow his audience to achieve his goals.

In addition to blogging, you might consider guest blogging, freelance blog writing, ghost blog writing, and other blog writing opportunities.

Monetization

A blogger can make money through several different methods. Here are some of the most common ways that bloggers monetize their content:

Advertising revenue: Bloggers can earn money by displaying ads on their websites. They can use advertising networks like Google AdSense or work directly with advertisers.

Affiliate marketing: Bloggers can earn a commission by promoting products or services in their blog posts and including affiliate links. When a reader clicks on the link and makes a purchase, the blogger earns a percentage of the sale.

Sponsored posts: Bloggers can earn money by writing posts that promote a product or service for a brand. They may receive a fee or free products in exchange for the sponsored post.

Selling digital products: Bloggers can create and sell digital products like e-books, courses, or printables. This can be a great way to earn passive income.

Offering services: Bloggers can provide consulting, coaching, or freelance writing services. This can be a good way to monetize their expertise.

Using ChatGPT

Content ideas: ChatGPT can provide ideas for new blog content based on a blogger's niche, audience, and interests. Bloggers can ask ChatGPT open-ended questions about their blog and get suggestions for new topics to cover.

Research: ChatGPT can help with research by answering questions on a wide range of topics. Bloggers can ask ChatGPT for information on specific subjects and receive relevant and accurate answers.

Writing prompts: ChatGPT can provide writing prompts for bloggers struggling with writer's block or needing inspiration for their next post or article.

Editing and proofreading: ChatGPT can help with editing and proofreading by suggesting changes to sentence structure, grammar, and punctuation.

SEO optimization: ChatGPT can help with SEO optimization by providing suggestions for blog titles, meta descriptions, and other metadata. Bloggers can ask ChatGPT questions about optimizing their blog posts for search engines and get helpful tips.

Prompt Examples

- "Write a detailed guide on SEO for beginners, providing valuable tips, advice, and resources."
- "Create a listicle of your top recommendations for books about making passive income."
- "Write a how-to post or tutorial on how to excel as a Fiverr seller."
- "Discuss the top 5 trends in blogging for 2023."
- "Write a comparison of the top hosting services for bloggers."

AI Tools for Bloggers

Quillbot is an AI paraphrasing tool that helps you rewrite sentences, paragraphs, or entire articles while maintaining the original meaning. This can be useful for improving your writing and avoiding plagiarism.

Copy.ai uses AI to generate creative copy for various purposes, including blog posts, headlines, social media captions, and more.

Rytr.me is an AI copywriting tool that helps you generate content for your blog posts, ad copy, product descriptions, and more based on specific keywords or topics.

Textmetrics.com is an AI-driven content optimization tool that helps you create SEO-friendly and high-quality content tailored to your target audience.

Spotlight: Jasper

BENEFITS OF JASPER

How will Jasper unlock your creative potential?

Image credit: Jasper

Jasper is an AI-powered platform that provides customer service automation solutions for businesses. It uses machine learning and natural language processing technologies to automate customer interactions across various channels, including email, chat, and voice. Jasper offers paid plans only.

Jasper's key features include the following:

- Boss Mode: Write long content like blog posts, reports, emails, and stories.
- Jasper Chat: Interact with AI in a natural dialog with an easy-to-use interface to generate content quickly.
- Art: Jasper creates amazing art in seconds for ads, thumbnails, illustrations, and more.
- Chrome extension: Add the Jasper Chrome extension to bring your AI assistant everywhere you work.
- Multiple languages: Jasper can read and write intelligent and creative content in over 29 languages.
- Surfer SEO Integration: Write optimized content five times faster for high rankings on Google.
- Real-time analytics: Jasper provides real-time analytics and insights into customer interactions, allowing

businesses to track performance and make data-driven decisions.

- Integrations: Jasper integrates with popular business tools and applications, such as Salesforce, Slack, and Zendesk, making it easy for businesses to incorporate customer service automation into their existing workflows.

Authors

Books have been around for centuries, so the authorship concept is familiar to most people. A book author is a person who writes books. Book authors can write in various genres, including fiction, non-fiction, poetry, memoirs, and more. They may write books for children, young adults, or adults and can work independently or as part of a publishing team.

Once a book is published, the author may participate in marketing and promotion efforts to increase awareness and drive sales. This may involve book signings, interviews, speaking engagements, and social media promotion.

Successful book authors typically have a strong command of language and writing, a creative imagination, and the ability to write compelling stories or convey complex information in an engaging and accessible way. They also need to have perseverance, as writing a book can be long and challenging.

Getting Started

Book authors typically go through several stages in the writing process, including research, outlining, writing, editing, and publishing. After that, they may work with an agent or editor to help them refine their work and find a publisher. Alternatively, they may self-publish their books on platforms like Amazon Kindle Direct Publishing (KDP).

Amazon KDP is a self-publishing platform that allows authors to publish their books in digital and physical formats and sell them on Amazon, one of the world's largest online marketplaces. KDP offers a range of tools and features that make it easy for authors to publish their books, set their prices, and market their work to a global audience. Once the book is published, it becomes available on Amazon's Kindle Store.

Amazon has a sizeable share of online book sales. Therefore, you'll likely waste your time trying to sell through alternatives like Google Play Books, Apple Books, Lulu, etc.

Image credit: Amazon KDP

Monetization

The amount of money earned by book authors can vary widely depending on factors such as the book's popularity, the author's contract, and their marketing efforts.

Here are some of the most common ways that book authors earn an income:

Royalties: When an author's book is sold, they earn a percentage of the sale price as a royalty. The royalty rate can vary depending on the publisher, the type of book, and the author's contract. For example, traditional publishers typically offer royalty rates between 7% and 25% of the sale price. In comparison, self-published authors can earn up to 70% of the sale price on platforms like Amazon Kindle Direct Publishing.

Advances: In some cases, traditional publishers may offer authors an advance on their royalties. This is a lump sum of money paid to the author upfront, with the expectation that the passage will be earned back through future book sales.

Speaking engagements: Successful authors may be invited to speak at conferences, bookstores, and other events, where they can earn speaking fees.

Book tours: Some authors may go on book tours to promote their books and meet readers. While book tours can be expensive, they can generate publicity and sales.

Film and TV adaptations: If an author's book is adapted into a movie or TV show, they may earn a one-time fee or ongoing royalties.

Using ChatGPT

Alongside brainstorming, overcoming writer's block, and inspiring new ideas, ChatGPT can help with fiction and nonfiction writing in several ways.

Fiction

Generating ideas: ChatGPT can help develop plot, character development, and settings ideas. In addition, users can ask ChatGPT open-ended questions about their story, and it can provide suggestions and ideas.

Character development: ChatGPT can help develop a character by answering questions about the character's backstory, personality traits, and motivations.

Nonfiction

Research: ChatGPT can help with research by providing answers to questions on a wide range of topics. Nonfiction writers can ask ChatGPT for information on specific subjects and receive relevant and accurate information.

Fact-checking: ChatGPT can help with fact-checking by providing accurate information on a topic. Nonfiction writers can verify data to ensure the accuracy of their work.

ChatGPT can help book authors with editing and proofreading by suggesting sentence structure, grammar, and punctuation changes.

Prompt Examples

- "Write the foundation for a short story or novel about cats chasing dogs."
- "Create a unique character and write a character profile, including their background, motivations, and inner demons."
- "Choose a historical event and write a fictional story set in that context, incorporating accurate details, an engaging plot, and a climax."
- "Write a scene where two characters with contrasting personalities have a meaningful conversation, highlighting their differences and similarities."
- "Describe an unusual setting and how it impacts the characters and events in my book about Irish elves."

AI Tools for Authors

ProWritingAid is a writing tool that uses AI to analyze writing and provide suggestions for improvements. It can help authors identify grammar and spelling errors, improve sentence structure, and enhance readability.

Scrivener is a tool that uses AI to help authors organize their writing projects. For example, it can help authors create outlines, organize research, and manage multiple drafts.

Copyscape.com is an AI-powered tool that can help authors detect plagiarism in their writing. It can compare a document to a database of web pages and highlight any matching text.

AutoCrit is a writing tool that uses AI to help authors improve their writing. For example, it can analyze and suggest pacing, dialogue, and descriptive writing improvements.

Spotlight: Grammarly

Great Writing, Simplified

Compose bold, clear, mistake-free writing with Grammarly's new AI-powered desktop Windows app.

Get Grammarly It's free

Image credit: Grammarly

Grammarly is a digital writing assistant that uses AI and natural language processing technology to help users improve their writing. It is available as a web-based application, a browser extension, and a mobile app. Free and paid plans are available.

Grammarly can benefit students, professionals, and non-native English speakers who want to improve their writing skills and avoid common mistakes. Grammarly's key features include the following:

Grammar and spelling checks: Grammarly can detect and correct grammatical and spelling mistakes in real-time as users type.

Writing suggestions: Grammarly offers tips for alternative words, sentence structure, and style to improve the overall clarity and effectiveness of writing.

Plagiarism checker: Grammarly can detect plagiarism by comparing a user's text to a database of over 16 billion web pages and academic papers.

Tone detector: Grammarly can analyze the tone of a user's writing and suggest adjustments to better match the intended style.

Vocabulary enhancement: Grammarly can suggest new vocabulary words to help users express their ideas more effectively.

Course Creators

Making money online by selling courses exploded when companies like Skillshare and Udemy launched in the early 2010s. That should come as no surprise since people love to or must learn to keep pace and upskill in an ever-changing world. Moreover, E-learning makes personal and professional development convenient, cost-efficient, flexible, and rewarding, lending itself to high industry growth prospects for years to come.

An online course instructor designs and teaches courses in an online learning environment. Online courses are typically delivered through a learning management system (LMS) or another platform. They can cover a wide range of topics, from academic subjects to professional development and personal growth.

Online course instructors play a critical role in providing accessible and high-quality education to students worldwide. They bring their expertise and passion to the online learning environment, creating courses that help students achieve their learning goals and advance their careers.

The duties of an online course instructor can vary depending on the specific course and the institution offering it. However, some typical responsibilities of online course instructors include the following:

- Develop course content: Online instructors create and develop course content, including lesson plans, instructional materials, and assessments. They may also select textbooks or other readings for the course.
- Deliver lectures and facilitate discussions: Online instructors deliver lessons, facilitate discussions, and provide feedback to students. They may do this through video conferencing, discussion forums, or other online tools.
- Provide feedback and assessment: Online course instructors grade assignments and provide feedback to

students on their progress. They may also hold office hours or provide one-on-one feedback to students who need extra help.

- Interact with students: Online course instructors interact with students through online platforms, answering questions and providing support as needed. They may also guide career or academic paths and help students navigate the course material.
- Stay current: Online course instructors stay current in their field and update their course content as needed. They may attend conferences, participate in professional development, or engage in research to keep current on the latest developments in their subject area.

Getting Started

First, each e-learning platform has unique requirements to teach. Secondly, thousands of teacher flock to Udemy, Skillshare, and similar course self-publishing platforms to sell and monetize their courses. If you're interested in teaching on Udemy, here are some steps to follow:

1. Choose your course topic: First, choose a topic for your course that you're knowledgeable and passionate about. Udemy offers classes on a wide range of subjects, so there are many opportunities to teach in your area of expertise.
2. Plan your course: Once you've chosen your course topic, plan your course content. Create a course outline that includes the topics you'll cover, the length of each lecture, and any supplementary materials you'll provide.
3. Create your course content: Next, create your course content. This can include video lectures, slide presentations, and written materials. You can use Udemy's course creation tools to record and upload your video lectures.

4. Publish your course: Once you've created your course content, publish your course on Udemy. You'll need to fill out some basic information about your course, including the title, description, and target audience.
5. Promote your course: Promote it once your class is published to attract students. You can use social media, email marketing, and other tactics to drive traffic to your course page.
6. Engage with your students: As students enroll in your course, engage with them through Udemy's discussion boards and messaging system. Answer questions and provide feedback to help your students succeed.
7. Update your course: Finally, update your course as needed to keep it up-to-date and relevant. You can use Udemy's analytics tools to track student engagement and identify areas for improvement.

The latest in learning

Stay on top of the skills you need. Log in for dea courses. Sale ends April 6.

Image credit: Udemy

Monetization

Here are some of the most common ways that online course instructors earn an income:

Selling courses: Online course instructors can sell their courses to students through various platforms, such as Udemy, Skillshare, or their websites. Instructors can set the price of their classes and earn revenue from each sale.

Subscriptions: Some online course instructors offer subscriptions to their courses, where students pay monthly fees for access to the course content. Instructors can earn recurring revenue from these subscriptions.

Consulting and coaching: Online course instructors may offer consulting or coaching services to students who need extra help or personalized attention. Instructors can charge a fee for these services, which can provide additional income.

Affiliate marketing: Online course instructors can earn commissions by promoting other courses or products related to their course topic. Instructors can include affiliate links in their course materials or on their websites and earn commissions on sales made through those links.

Sponsorships: Online course instructors may also earn money through sponsorships. Companies may sponsor a course or offer to pay the instructor for promoting their products or services.

Using ChatGPT

ChatGPT can be a helpful tool for online course instructors looking to improve their course content, optimize their course for the LMS algorithm, and attract more students. For instance, ChatGPT can help with research and course optimization by providing suggestions for lecture titles, descriptions, and other metadata.

Instructors can also ask ChatGPT questions about optimizing their course for the LMS algorithm and get helpful suggestions.

Prompt Examples

- "Create a short guide about student interaction and community-building for my online course."
- "Create an outline for my course about training dogs."
- "Write an introduction for an online class about losing belly fat."
- "Write a description for my course about yoga for beginners."
- "Write about strategies for staying motivated and productive as an online course instructor."

AI Tools for Online Course Instructors

AI tools for online course instructors are limited to video recording and editing software. So, teachers can use the same AI tools as other video and content creators.

5. MAKE MONEY ONLINE WITH E-COMMERCE

In speaking with various digital entrepreneurs, making money in e-commerce seems to be one of the most desirable activities. Success stories constantly float around on venture funding shows like Shark Tank and Dragon' Den to justify people's excitement.

According to Shopify (Global E-commerce Explained: Stats and Trends to Watch),

"The global e-commerce market is expected to total $5.7 trillion in 2022. That figure is estimated to grow over the next few years, showing that borderless e-commerce is becoming a profitable option for online retailers.

Two years ago, only 17.8% of sales were made from online purchases. That number is expected to reach 20.8% in 2023, a 2 percentage point increase in e-commerce market share. Growth is expected to continue, reaching 23% by 2025, which translates to a 5.2 percentage point increase in just five years."

Leading the Way

China is the largest e-commerce market in the world. The rapid growth of internet users, widespread adoption of mobile devices, and improvements in digital payment systems have fueled the expansion of its e-commerce industry. In second place is the United States, with its robust middle class and technological innovation led by companies like Amazon. Some leading global e-commerce companies include:

Alibaba Group—Founded by Jack Ma in 1999, Alibaba is a Chinese e-commerce giant that operates various online marketplaces, including Alibaba.com (B2B), Taobao (C2C), and Tmall (B2C). It has a massive presence in China and is expanding its reach in other countries.

Amazon—Founded by Jeff Bezos in 1994, Amazon is the largest e-commerce company globally, with a dominant presence in North America, Europe, and many other regions. It offers a vast range of products and services, including consumer electronics, apparel, groceries, and digital content.

eBay—eBay is a US-based e-commerce company primarily operating as an online auction and shopping platform. It enables individuals and businesses to buy and sell various products and services worldwide.

JD.com—Another Chinese e-commerce company, JD.com, is known for its wide selection of products, extensive logistics network, and focus on product authenticity. It mainly operates in China but is also extending its reach to other markets.

Shopify—A Canadian e-commerce platform, Shopify, allows businesses to create online stores and manage products, inventory, and payments. It has become standard for small and medium-sized businesses looking to establish an online presence.

Walmart—Although primarily known as a brick-and-mortar retailer, Walmart has significantly expanded its e-commerce operations in recent years, offering a wide range of products online and investing in acquisitions and partnerships to strengthen its digital presence.

E-Commerce Sellers

Starting a retail e-commerce business involves several fundamental steps, from choosing a niche to setting up an online store and marketing your products. Here's a guide to help you get started:

Choose a niche: Identify a specific market or product category you're passionate about and know about. Then, conduct market research to assess demand, competition, and potential profitability.

Define your target audience: Understand your potential customers' needs, preferences, and demographics to tailor your product offerings and marketing strategies.

Select products: Choose the products you want to sell based on your niche, target audience, and market research. Consider factors such as pricing, quality, and differentiation from competitors.

Determine your business model: Decide whether you want to sell your products using a dropshipping model, manufacture or source products yourself, or partner with a wholesaler. Each model has pros and cons, so carefully consider which suits your resources and objectives best.

Choose a platform: Select an e-commerce platform like Shopify, WooCommerce, BigCommerce, or Magento to build your online store. Consider factors such as ease of use, pricing, available features, and scalability. Alternatively, create an account and sell on online marketplaces like Amazon and ebay.

Create your online store: Design your website, considering user experience, branding, and responsiveness. You may need to learn some web design basics or hire a professional web designer to help create an attractive and functional store.

Set up payment and shipping options: Integrate payment gateways like PayPal, Stripe, or Square to process transactions securely. Determine your shipping strategy, including carriers, shipping zones, and pricing.

Manage inventory and order fulfillment: Keep track of your inventory levels, order processing, and shipping logistics. Alternatively, if you use a dropshipping model, partner with reliable suppliers that can fulfill orders promptly and accurately.

Set up legal and tax requirements: Register your business, obtain necessary licenses and permits, and set up sales tax collection in compliance with local and international regulations.

Market your business: Promote your online store through various marketing channels, such as social media, email marketing, search engine optimization (SEO), content marketing, and paid advertising.

Monitor and optimize: Regularly analyze your store's performance using analytics tools, customer feedback, and sales data. Then, adjust your website design, product offerings, and marketing strategies to improve customer experience and increase sales.

Amazon FBA

How FBA works

Amazon FBA can help decrease fulfillment headaches as you scal

Step 1: **Set up FBA**

Create your Amazon selling account, and login to Seller Central to set

Step 2: **Create product listings**

Once you add products to the Amazon catalog, specify FBA inventory

Step 3: **Prepare products**

Prepare the products for safe and secure transportation to a fulfillme guidelines and shipping and routing requirements.

Step 4: **Ship products to Amazon**

Create a shipping plan, print Amazon shipment ID labels, and send sh Learn more about sending inventory to Amazon.

Image credit: Amazon FBA

Starting an independent e-commerce store can be a daunting task for beginners. So, many sellers sell on Amazon using Amazon FBA.

Amazon FBA, or Fulfillment by Amazon, is a service provided by Amazon that allows sellers to store their products in Amazon's fulfillment centers. Amazon takes care of these products' storage, packaging, shipping, and customer service, making it easier for sellers to manage their inventory and orders.

When a customer orders a product fulfilled by Amazon, Amazon picks, packs, and ships the product on behalf of the seller. In addition, Amazon handles any returns and customer inquiries related to the order, providing a seamless experience for sellers and customers.

Using Amazon FBA can offer several benefits to sellers, including:

- Time savings: Amazon takes care of the logistics, freeing up sellers' time to focus on other aspects of their business, such as marketing and product sourcing.
- Access to Prime customers: Products fulfilled by Amazon are eligible for Amazon Prime, giving sellers access to a large and loyal customer base that values fast and reliable shipping.
- Increased visibility: FBA products often rank higher in Amazon search results, increasing the chances of customers finding and purchasing the products.
- Trust and credibility: Since Amazon handles shipping and customer service, customers may feel more confident purchasing from FBA sellers as they trust the Amazon brand.
- Global reach: Amazon FBA allows sellers to tap into Amazon's international marketplaces and fulfillment network, expanding their reach to customers worldwide.

However, using Amazon FBA also comes with some costs, such as storage fees, fulfillment fees, and additional charges for long-term storage. Therefore, sellers must carefully evaluate these costs and consider whether Amazon FBA is a suitable option for their business.

Making Money

E-commerce retailers generate sales from the products they sell. Their profits depend on various costs, such as the cost of goods sold (COGS), customer acquisition costs (CAC), and overhead.

Using ChatGPT

A CNBC article, "Amazon sellers are using ChatGPT to help write product listings in sprawling marketplace," described how Amazon retailers are taking advantage of ChatGPT to grow their businesses:

"Chad Rubin was looking for a way to spice up his Amazon listing for a vacuum hose. He was struggling to come up with a catchy title that would make shoppers want to click on his hose instead of the countless others in Amazon's vast marketplace.

For assistance, Rubin turned to ChatGPT, the artificial intelligence chatbot that's gone viral since its launch late last year. He soon began to experiment with the tool for completing tasks such as generating copy on his product page. Rubin asked ChatGPT to "generate 5 insanely clever and catchy headlines" for an infographic promoting his vacuum cleaner hose."

Here are some ways in which ChatGPT can help e-commerce sellers:

Product Descriptions—ChatGPT can generate compelling and informative product descriptions that highlight the key features and benefits of the items, making them more appealing to potential buyers.

Marketing Content—E-commerce sellers can use ChatGPT to create engaging marketing materials, such as email newsletters, social media posts, and blog articles, to promote their products and brand.

FAQ Creation—ChatGPT can help sellers generate a comprehensive list of frequently asked questions (FAQs) and corresponding answers, addressing common customer concerns and inquiries.

Customer Support—By integrating ChatGPT into a chatbot, e-commerce sellers can provide real-time customer support, answering questions and resolving issues efficiently, reducing the need for manual intervention.

Product Recommendations—ChatGPT can suggest relevant products to customers based on their preferences, purchase history, or browsing behavior, enhancing the shopping experience and potentially increasing sales.

Content Optimization—ChatGPT can help sellers optimize their content for search engines, providing suggestions for keywords, meta descriptions, and other SEO elements to improve their store's visibility and organic traffic.

Inventory Planning—Sellers can use ChatGPT to analyze historical sales data and generate forecasts for future demand, helping them make informed decisions about inventory management.

Competitive Analysis—ChatGPT can assist sellers in identifying their competition, analyzing their strengths and weaknesses, and suggesting strategies to differentiate themselves in the market.

Business Planning—E-commerce sellers can leverage ChatGPT to create business plans, outlining goals, strategies, and key performance indicators (KPIs), which can help them stay organized and focused on their objectives.

Training Materials—ChatGPT can generate employee training materials and guides covering customer service, order fulfillment, and store management.

Prompt Examples

- "Share five strategies for providing exceptional customer experiences."
- "How can I promote my fashion products on YouTube?"
- "Write a 200-word product description for my gender-neutral nail polish products."
- "What details or criteria should I include in a comparison article about lead generation apps?"
- "Provide ten relevant keywords for facial cream products."

AI Tools for App Developers

E-commerce AI tools come in and go out of the market quickly. So, searching for "e-commerce AI tools" and "the best e-commerce AI tools" is advisable to find current and in-demand apps. In the meantime, here are some of the best AI tools for e-commerce sellers.

Klevu is an AI-powered site search tool that provides personalized and relevant search results, improving the shopping experience for customers and potentially increasing sales.

ReSci, or Retention Science, is an AI-powered customer data platform that uses predictive analytics to optimize email marketing campaigns, customer segmentation, and personalization, helping sellers improve customer retention and lifetime value.

Conversica is an AI-driven sales assistant that automates lead engagement and follow-up, helping e-commerce sellers nurture and convert leads more efficiently.

AdScale.com is an AI-powered platform that optimizes e-commerce sellers' advertising campaigns across multiple channels, such as Google, Facebook, and Instagram, improving ad performance and ROI.

Gorgias is an AI-powered customer support platform that helps e-commerce sellers manage customer inquiries and issues efficiently, reducing response times and improving customer satisfaction.

Vue.ai is an AI-based visual intelligence platform that offers automated product tagging, personalized product recommendations, and visual search capabilities, enhancing customer experiences and streamlining operations.

Bluecore is a retail marketing platform that uses AI to optimize email marketing, on-site product recommendations, and audience targeting, helping e-commerce sellers increase customer engagement and drive sales.

Spotlight: Shopify

Image credit: Shopify

Shopify is a leading e-commerce platform allowing individuals and businesses to create and manage their online stores easily. Founded in 2006 by Tobias Lütke, Daniel Weinand, and Scott Lake, Shopify has grown to become one of the most popular e-commerce solutions globally, catering to businesses of all sizes.

Shopify offers a range of features and tools to help users set up, customize, and manage their online stores, including:

Store builder: A user-friendly interface with customizable themes and templates to design the look and feel of your online store without requiring extensive coding knowledge.

Product management: A comprehensive system to manage products, track inventory, and organize products into collections, making it easy for customers to browse and shop.

Payment processing: Integration with various payment gateways, such as Shopify Payments, PayPal, and Stripe, allows you to accept customer payments securely and efficiently.

Shipping management: Tools to set up shipping options, calculate rates, and print shipping labels, as well as integration with popular carriers like UPS, FedEx, and USPS.

Sales channels: The ability to sell products through multiple channels, including social media platforms, online marketplaces, and brick-and-mortar stores.

Marketing tools: Built-in features for search engine optimization (SEO), email marketing, and social media marketing, as well as integration with various marketing apps.

Reporting and analytics: Comprehensive reporting and analytics tools to monitor store performance, customer behavior, and sales trends, helping you make informed decisions about your business.

App Store: Access to the Shopify App Store, which offers a wide range of third-party apps designed to enhance various aspects of your e-commerce business, such as customer support, inventory management, and marketing.

Customer support: 24/7 customer support through chat, email, and phone, as well as access to a vast knowledge base and community forums.

Shopify offers different pricing plans to cater to businesses of various sizes and requirements, from small companies and startups to large enterprises.

Shopify offers free tools, online courses, and hundreds of resources to help sellers succeed.

AI Tool

Shopify Magic uses AI to help merchants generate product descriptions. Merchants enter a few keywords to target in search results, select a tone (like "novice" or "expert"), and Shopify Magic does the rest. The result will be high-quality, compelling product descriptions that take seconds to create, helping sellers to save time, sell more, and get their products in front of more shoppers.

Spotlight: Jungle Scout

JungleScout Solutions ⌄ Features ⌄ Pricing Resourc

AI Assist is here! Jungle Scout's new integration with OpenAI

Start and scale your ecommerce business

Image credit: Jungle Scout

Jungle Scout is a popular software suite designed for Amazon sellers to help them research products, find profitable niches, and optimize their product listings. It offers a range of tools and resources to assist in various aspects of selling on Amazon, including:

Product Database: Jungle Scout's product database allows sellers to search for and filter products based on specific criteria, such as category, estimated sales, revenue, and more. This helps sellers identify profitable products and niches to target.

Product Tracker: This feature helps sellers track the performance of products over time, including sales, revenue, and inventory levels. It assists sellers in monitoring the competition and making informed decisions about their product offerings.

Keyword Scout: Jungle Scout's keyword research tool provides data on search volume, competition, and recommended PPC bids for relevant keywords. This helps sellers optimize their product listings for search visibility and improve their Amazon SEO.

Supplier Database: The supplier database enables sellers to find and verify suppliers for their products. It offers information about the supplier's shipments, customers, and products, helping sellers make more informed decisions about their supply chain.

Sales Analytics: Jungle Scout's sales analytics feature helps sellers track and analyze their sales data, including revenue, profits, and expenses. This allows them to make data-driven decisions to optimize their business operations.

Listing Builder: The listing builder feature assists sellers in creating optimized product listings by providing keyword suggestions and real-time feedback on the listing's quality.

Academy and Resources: Jungle Scout also offers educational resources, such as tutorials, webinars, and case studies, to help sellers learn more about selling on Amazon and using the Jungle Scout tools effectively.

AI Tool

AI Assist is a powerful AI integration to Jungle Scout that can write instant product listing copy for Amazon sellers. It uses Jungle Scout's lists of relevant and competitive Amazon keywords and leverages OpenAI's model to generate listing copy, including a title, description, and more.

Discover my favorite online business and marketing apps: https://subscribepage.io/mike-reuben

6. MAKE MONEY ONLINE WITH DIGITAL MARKETING

What do Alphabet (Google and YouTube), Meta (Facebook and Instagram), Amazon, and Microsoft have in common? Aside from being some of the largest global tech companies by market capitalization, they generate billions in advertising revenue. So, while digital marketing could fit into a chapter about freelance services, it's worthy of a chapter to cover the many opportunities available.

A digital marketer designs, implements, and manages marketing campaigns and strategies using digital channels and platforms to promote a brand, product, or service. Their main objective is to increase brand awareness, generate leads, drive website traffic, and boost sales.

Getting Started – All Digital Marketing Roles

To get started as a digital marketer, one should develop a strong foundation in digital marketing principles, learn about various digital channels, and gain hands-on experience. Here are some areas to focus on:

Learn the fundamentals: Acquire a basic understanding of marketing principles and concepts. While a formal degree in marketing or a related field is beneficial, it's not always necessary. There are numerous online courses, certifications, and resources available that can help you build a strong foundation in digital marketing. Then, as you progress in your career, continue to learn and grow by taking advanced courses, attending workshops, and staying informed about industry developments. This will help you remain competitive and adapt to the ever-changing digital marketing landscape.

Learn the tools and platforms: Familiarize yourself with popular digital marketing tools and platforms, such as Google Analytics, Google Ads, Facebook Ads Manager, email marketing software, content management systems (CMS), and social media management tools.

Acquire relevant skills: Develop skills in areas like search engine optimization (SEO), content marketing, social media marketing, email marketing, pay-per-click (PPC) advertising, and analytics. You may choose to specialize in one or more of these areas, but having a broad understanding of all aspects is beneficial.

Get certified: Obtain certifications from reputable organizations or platforms like Google, Facebook, or HubSpot, which can help validate your skills and enhance your credibility as a digital marketer.

Build an online presence: Create a personal website, blog, or portfolio to showcase your digital marketing skills, knowledge, and projects. Engage with the digital marketing community on social media, forums, or online groups to learn from others and build your network.

Gain hands-on experience: Apply your digital marketing skills by working on real projects, either through internships, freelance work, or helping local businesses and non-profit organizations. This hands-on experience is invaluable for refining your skills and building a portfolio.

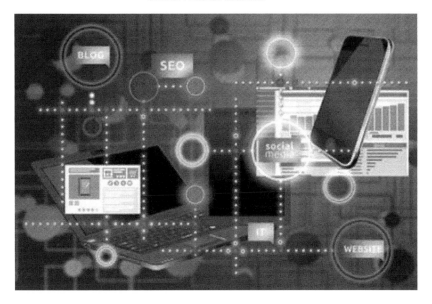

Image credit: Gerd Altmann from Pixabay

Making Money – All Digital Marketing Roles

Digital marketers can make money through various channels, depending on their skills, experience, and chosen career path. Here are some ways digital marketers can earn money:

Employment—Many digital marketers work as full-time employees in companies, agencies, or organizations. They may have specific roles such as SEO specialist, social media manager, content marketer, or digital marketing strategist. Salaries vary depending on the position, experience, industry, and location.

Freelance work—Some digital marketers choose to work as freelancers, providing their services to clients on a project-by-project basis. Freelancers can earn money by offering content creation, social media management, website design, or PPC campaign management. The income for freelancers may vary based on the number of clients, project scope, and expertise.

75

Consulting—Experienced digital marketers may offer consulting services to businesses, helping them develop and implement digital marketing strategies, analyze campaign performance, and optimize their online presence. Consultants usually charge hourly or project-based fees.

Agency—Digital marketers with entrepreneurial ambitions can establish a digital marketing agency, providing a range of services to clients, such as SEO, social media marketing, content marketing, and more. Agency owners can generate revenue through client fees, retainers, or performance-based contracts.

Online courses and workshops—Digital marketers with solid teaching skills can create and sell online courses, workshops, or webinars, sharing their knowledge and expertise with others looking to learn digital marketing. This can generate passive income through course sales or paid webinars.

Affiliate marketing—Digital marketers can earn money through affiliate marketing by promoting products or services of other companies and earning a commission for each sale made through their unique referral links. This can be done through a blog, social media, or other platforms.

Sponsored content and partnerships—A digital marketer with a robust online presence or following can earn money through sponsored content or partnerships with brands. This may include creating sponsored blog posts and social media content or hosting sponsored events or webinars.

Monetize a blog or website—Digital marketers who run blogs or websites can generate income through various monetization strategies, such as display advertising, sponsored content, or selling digital products like e-books or templates.

Using ChatGPT – All Digital Marketing Roles

Content creation: ChatGPT can help generate ideas for blog posts, social media content, email marketing copy, or ad headlines. It can also help create draft content or provide suggestions for improvements, making the content creation process more efficient.

Keyword research: ChatGPT can suggest relevant keywords and phrases related to a specific topic or niche. This can assist digital marketers in optimizing their content for search engines and improving their SEO efforts.

Brainstorming: Digital marketers can use ChatGPT to brainstorm ideas for marketing campaigns, promotional strategies, or creative concepts. The AI can provide a range of suggestions based on prompts, helping marketers think outside the box and develop innovative campaigns.

Competitor analysis: ChatGPT can help digital marketers analyze competitors by summarizing website content, identifying key features or offerings, and providing insights into their marketing strategies.

Social media engagement: Digital marketers can use ChatGPT to draft responses to comments or messages on social media platforms, making maintaining an active and engaged online presence easier.

Optimization suggestions: Digital marketers can use ChatGPT to get tips for campaign optimization, such as testing different bidding strategies, targeting options, or ad placements.

Reporting and analysis: ChatGPT can help digital marketers create concise and informative reports summarizing campaign results, highlighting key insights, and identifying areas for improvement.

A/B testing ideas: ChatGPT can assist digital marketers in generating ideas for A/B testing, such as variations in ad copy, design, or landing page elements to optimize campaign performance.

Research assistance: Digital marketers can use ChatGPT to gather information on specific topics, trends, or industry developments, helping them stay informed and up to date with the latest news and insights.

Prompt Examples – All Digital Marketing Roles

- "Develop a chatbot script for a customer service representative to handle frequently asked questions and concerns."
- "Compare the best affiliate networks to join in the United States?"
- "Generate a compelling headline and meta description for a new blog post about the latest digital marketing trends."
- "Create a social media post that maximizes engagement and reach for my new blue lipstick product."
- "Develop a personalized email marketing campaign for my Indian-based customers for fashion products."
- "Provide me with a template to help identify and track nano-influencers for my new product launch."
- "Generate a list of blog title ideas for content about iron supplements."
- "Create a personalized birthday message for customers on their special day."
- "Create a list of 10 keywords to use in my Google Ads campaign for Halloween costumes."
- "Write a two-sentence ad for a new line of organic orange juice."

Introducing Nature's Nectar Organic Orange Juice, the purest way to start your day! Made from sun-kissed, handpicked oranges and free of artificial additives, our juice delivers an invigorating burst of natural flavor that'll leave you feeling refreshed and revitalized.

Image credit: OpenAI

- "Create a compelling email subject line for an upcoming winter sale."
- "Develop a 4-part welcome email series for new subscribers to my cooking recipe blog."
- "Write a persuasive email about the benefits of conversion rate optimization."
- "Write a post-purchase follow-up email to encourage customers to leave reviews."
- "Create a marketing campaign for a new line of sustainable bamboo pillows."
- "Write a product description for a new type of electric bike."
- "Develop a sales funnel for a new online course that teaches people how to start their own Shopify store."
- "Write an outline for a post about the best lead generation strategies."
- "Give me a list of alternatives to Google Ads.
- "Provide 15 hashtags for my fitness challenge on TikTok."

Performance Marketers

A performance marketer focuses on designing, executing, and optimizing marketing campaigns with a primary emphasis on achieving measurable results or performance metrics. The primary goal of a performance marketer is to drive specific actions, such as sales, leads, app downloads, or user registrations, while maximizing return on investment (ROI) and minimizing cost per action (CPA).

Key Responsibilities

Campaign strategy: Performance marketers develop and plan marketing strategies based on a target audience, marketing objectives, and budget. They identify the most suitable marketing channels, targeting options, and creatives to achieve the desired results.

Campaign execution: Performance marketers set up, launch, and manage marketing campaigns across various channels, including search engine marketing (SEM), social media advertising, display advertising, native advertising, and affiliate marketing.

Optimization: Performance marketers continuously monitor and analyze campaign performance data, making real-time adjustments to targeting, bidding, ad creatives, and landing pages to improve the efficiency and effectiveness of their campaigns.

Performance analysis: They use various analytics tools and platforms to track and measure the success of their campaigns, focusing on key performance indicators (KPIs) such as clicks, conversions, CPA, ROI, and customer lifetime value (CLTV).

Reporting: Performance marketers create regular reports to communicate campaign results to stakeholders, highlighting insights, achievements, and areas for improvement.

A/B testing: They frequently conduct A/B tests on ad creatives, targeting options, landing pages, and other campaign elements to identify the best-performing variations and optimize overall performance.

AI Tools for Performance Marketers

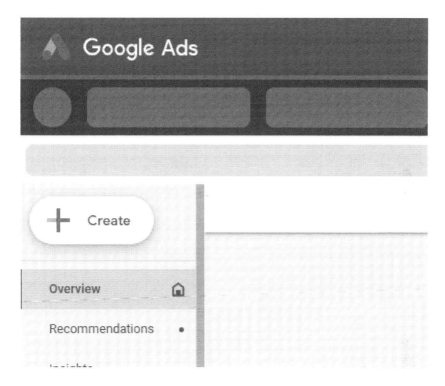

Image credit: Google Ads

Google's advertising platform incorporates AI and machine learning algorithms to optimize ad targeting, bidding, and placement. Features such as Smart Bidding and responsive search ads can help performance marketers drive better results more efficiently.

Facebook's advertising platform also uses AI to optimize ad delivery, targeting, and bidding. Dynamic ads, lookalike audiences, and automated ad testing are some features that can help performance marketers improve their campaign outcomes.

Albert.ai is an AI-powered marketing platform that automates and optimizes digital advertising campaigns across multiple channels, including search, social, and display. It can help performance marketers save time and improve results by making real-time adjustments based on data-driven insights.

Adext.ai is an AI-powered ad optimization platform that uses machine learning to automate audience targeting, bidding, and budget allocation for digital advertising campaigns. As a result, it helps performance marketers improve their ad performance and achieve better ROIs.

Phrasee.co is an AI-powered copywriting tool that generates and optimizes marketing copy for email, social media, and other channels. It can help performance marketers create persuasive and high-performing content to drive conversions.

Optmyzr is an AI-driven PPC management platform that provides advanced optimization tools and automation features for Google Ads and Microsoft Advertising campaigns. It can help performance marketers improve their ad performance and save time on campaign management tasks.

Revealbot is an AI-powered ad automation and reporting tool for Facebook, Instagram, and Google Ads. It offers features like automated rules, bulk ad creation, and performance alerts, which can help performance marketers manage and optimize their campaigns more effectively.

SEO Specialists

An SEO (Search Engine Optimization) specialist or expert focuses on optimizing websites and online content to improve their visibility and rankings in search engine results. The primary goal of an SEO is to drive organic (non-paid) traffic to a website by enhancing its visibility on search engines like Google, Bing, or Yahoo.

Key Responsibilities

Keyword research: Identifying relevant and high-value keywords that users will likely search for when looking for products, services, or information related to a website's niche or industry.

On-page optimization: Improving website elements such as title tags, meta descriptions, header tags, URL structure, and internal linking to make the site more search engine-friendly and to provide a better user experience.

Content optimization: Ensuring that the website content is well-organized, easily readable, and rich in relevant keywords while maintaining a natural flow and providing value to the users.

Technical SEO: Addressing technical aspects of the website, such as site speed, mobile responsiveness, site architecture, and structured data, to ensure optimal performance and indexing by search engines.

Off-page optimization: Building high-quality backlinks from authoritative and relevant websites to improve a site's domain authority, trustworthiness, and overall search engine ranking.

Local SEO: Optimizing a website for local search results by creating and managing local business listings, optimizing Google My Business profiles, and building local citations and reviews.

SEO audit: Analyzing a website's current SEO status, identifying areas of improvement, and providing recommendations to enhance search engine visibility and rankings.

Monitoring and reporting: Regularly tracking and analyzing website traffic, rankings, and user behavior through tools like Google Analytics and Google Search Console. Also, they create reports to communicate performance metrics and insights to stakeholders.

Staying updated: SEO is a constantly evolving field, and it's essential for SEO specialists to stay informed about the latest trends, algorithm updates, and best practices to maintain and improve their website's search engine performance.

AI Tools for SEO Specialist

Clearscope.io is a content optimization platform that utilizes AI to provide keyword research, content analysis, and optimization recommendations. It helps SEO specialists create content that is both relevant to their target audience and optimized for search engines.

Surfer SEO is an AI-powered on-page optimization tool that analyzes and compares content with top-ranking competitors, offering suggestions for keyword usage, content structure, and other on-page factors to improve search engine rankings.

Frase.io is an AI-driven content research and optimization tool that helps SEO specialists create more relevant content by identifying essential topics and keywords, analyzing competing content, and providing optimization recommendations.

Moz Pro is a comprehensive SEO suite that includes AI-powered features like keyword research, site crawl, and content optimization. It helps SEO specialists track their website's performance, identify issues, and uncover opportunities to improve search engine visibility.

BrightEdge is an AI-driven SEO and content marketing platform that provides insights and recommendations for keyword research, on-page optimization, and content strategy. It enables SEO specialists to create data-driven strategies and optimize their websites for maximum search visibility.

WordLift.io is an AI-powered SEO plugin for WordPress that helps optimize content by adding structured data, providing content recommendations, and improving internal linking. In addition, it assists SEO specialists in making their websites more accessible to search engines and enhancing user experience.

Social Media Marketers

A social media marketer specializes in promoting and managing brands, products, or services across various social media platforms, such as Facebook, Instagram, Twitter, LinkedIn, and more. Their primary goal is to increase brand awareness, engage with target audiences, drive traffic to websites, and ultimately convert followers or users into customers.

Key Responsibilities

Strategy development: Creating and implementing a comprehensive social media marketing strategy based on business goals, target audience, and budget while identifying the most suitable platforms and content types for each campaign.

Content creation: Producing engaging and relevant content tailored to each social media platform, such as images, videos, articles, and polls, to attract and retain followers while encouraging interaction and sharing.

Scheduling and posting: Managing a content calendar, scheduling, and publishing posts consistently, and ensuring timely responses to comments and messages from users.

Community management: Monitoring, moderating, and engaging with the online community to foster a positive brand image, respond to feedback, and address customer queries or complaints.

Analytics and reporting: Tracking and analyzing social media performance metrics, such as engagement, reach, and conversions, to evaluate campaign effectiveness and adjust strategies accordingly. Regularly reporting results to stakeholders and providing insights for future campaigns.

Advertising: Creating, managing, and optimizing paid social media advertising campaigns, targeting the right audience segments, and allocating budget efficiently to maximize ROI.

Influencer marketing: Identifying, connecting with, and managing relationships with relevant influencers or brand ambassadors to collaborate on campaigns, amplify brand reach, and enhance credibility.

Trend monitoring: Staying informed about the latest social media trends, platform updates, and emerging technologies to leverage new opportunities and maintain a competitive edge.

Cross-functional collaboration: Working closely with other teams, such as content, design, PR, and customer support, to ensure a cohesive and consistent brand message across all social media channels and campaigns.

AI Tools for Social Media Marketers

 Tools ∨   Channel:

Grow your audience on social and beyond

Buffer helps you build an audience organically. We're a values-driven company that provides affordable, intuitive, marketing tools for ambitious people and teams.

Image credit: Buffer

Buffer is a popular social media management tool that allows marketers to schedule, publish, and analyze content across multiple social media platforms. It simplifies content planning and helps maintain a consistent posting schedule.

Hootsuite is a comprehensive social media management platform that enables marketers to manage multiple social media accounts, schedule posts, monitor mentions, engage with followers, and analyze performance – all from one dashboard.

Sprout Social is an all-in-one social media management platform that offers scheduling, publishing, analytics, and engagement tools. It also provides features for managing social media advertising campaigns and customer support via social channels.

SocialBee is a social media management tool that helps marketers schedule and recycle evergreen content, categorize content, and analyze performance. It can also help grow and engage the audience through features like auto-follow and auto-reply.

BuzzSumo is a content research and analysis tool that helps social media marketers discover trending topics, high-performing content, and influential creators in their niche. In addition, it can help identify content ideas and understand what resonates with the target audience.

CRO Specialists

A Conversion Rate Optimization (CRO) specialist focuses on improving the performance of websites, landing pages, and other digital assets to increase the percentage of visitors who complete desired actions, such as making a purchase, signing up for a newsletter, or filling out a form. Their ultimate goal is to maximize conversions and boost the return on investment (ROI) of marketing efforts.

Key Responsibilities

Data Analysis: CRO specialists analyze a website and user behavior data to identify areas of improvement and potential bottlenecks that may hinder conversion rates.

A/B Testing and Multivariate Testing: They design and implement controlled experiments, such as A/B tests and multivariate tests, to compare different variations of webpages or elements and determine which version performs best regarding conversions.

User Experience (UX) Optimization: CRO specialists work on improving the overall user experience by optimizing website design, navigation, layout, and content, ensuring that visitors can easily find and complete the desired actions.

Website Personalization: They may develop personalized content and experiences for different user segments to increase engagement and conversion rates.

Copywriting and Messaging: CRO specialists often collaborate with copywriters and marketers to create compelling headlines, calls-to-action, and other content that resonates with the target audience and drives conversions.

Usability Testing: They conduct usability tests to gather insights on how real users interact with a website or digital asset, identifying pain points and opportunities for improvement.

Performance Analysis and Reporting: CRO specialists track and measure the effectiveness of their optimization efforts, reporting on key performance indicators (KPIs) and making data-driven recommendations for future improvements.

AI Tools for CRO Specialists

Google Analytics (with AI Insights): Google Analytics is a popular web analytics tool that helps track and analyze website traffic. Its AI-powered insights can automatically detect trends and anomalies, providing valuable information for CRO specialists to make data-driven decisions.

Optimizely is an experimentation platform that uses AI to help businesses test, personalize, and optimize their digital experiences. It offers A/B testing, multivariate testing, and personalization features, enabling CRO specialists to maximize conversion rates.

Unbounce is a landing page builder and optimization platform that uses AI to assist with creating high-converting landing pages. Its Smart Traffic feature automatically directs visitors to the most relevant version of a page, while the AI-powered Conversion Intelligence feature helps optimize landing pages for better performance.

VWO is an AI-driven conversion optimization platform that offers A/B testing, multivariate testing, and website personalization. In addition, its AI-powered SmartStats feature helps users make data-driven decisions about their tests.

DynamicYield.com is a personalization platform that uses machine learning to deliver tailored experiences to individual users. Additionally, it offers CRO specialists features like A/B testing, multivariate testing, and predictive targeting to improve conversion rates.

Instapage is a landing page builder and optimization platform that uses AI to help businesses create high-converting landing pages. Its AdMap feature enables users to visualize and connect ads to relevant post-click landing pages. At the same time, the Thor Render Engine ensures fast-loading pages for better user experience and conversion rates.

Content Marketers

A content marketer is responsible for strategizing, creating, distributing, and promoting valuable, relevant, and consistent content to attract, engage, and retain a clearly defined audience. Their goal is to drive profitable customer action, build brand awareness, and establish trust and authority within a specific industry or niche.

Key Responsibilities

Content strategy development: Creating a comprehensive content marketing strategy that aligns with the business goals, target audience, and brand voice while identifying the most suitable formats and channels for each campaign.

Content creation: Producing high-quality, engaging, and relevant content in various formats, such as blog posts, articles, videos, podcasts, infographics, e-books, whitepapers, and social media updates, to inform, entertain, or educate the target audience.

Content optimization: Ensuring content is optimized for search engines and user experience, incorporating relevant keywords, using proper formatting, and implementing SEO best practices.

Content distribution: Promoting and distributing content across various channels, such as social media, email marketing, paid advertising, and content syndication platforms, to reach the target audience and maximize visibility.

Audience engagement: Encouraging interaction and engagement with the content by responding to comments, answering questions, and fostering discussions around the topics covered.

Analytics and reporting: Tracking and analyzing content performance metrics, such as website traffic, engagement, conversions, and social shares, to evaluate campaign effectiveness and adjust strategies accordingly. Also, they regularly report results to stakeholders and provide insights for future content creation.

Content audit: Regularly reviewing and evaluating existing content to identify areas for improvement, updating outdated information, and removing or repurposing underperforming content.

AI Tools for Content Marketers

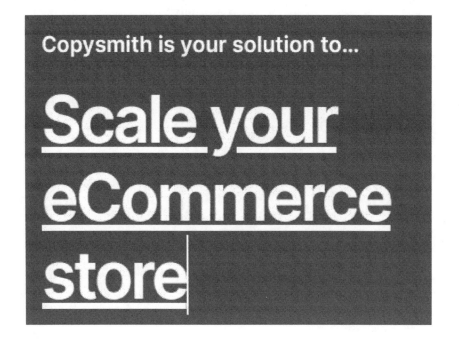

Image credit: Copysmith

Copysmith.ai is an AI-powered copywriting tool that can generate various types of content, such as blog posts, social media updates, ad copy, and product descriptions. It helps content marketers save time and effort in the content creation process.

MarketMuse is an AI-driven content planning and optimization tool that helps identify content gaps, conduct keyword research, and create high-quality, SEO content. It uses natural language processing (NLP) to analyze and score content based on relevance, authority, and user intent.

INK is an AI-powered writing editor specifically designed for SEO optimization. It helps bloggers create content that ranks higher on search engines by providing keyword suggestions, readability scores, and other optimization tips.

Outranking.io is an AI-powered content optimization tool that provides real-time suggestions for improving content quality, relevance, and search engine optimization. It helps content marketers create content that ranks higher in search engine results.

Contentdrips is an AI-powered content design tool that helps content marketers create visually appealing social media graphics, videos, and animations, simplifying the design process and saving time.

Email Marketers

An email marketer specializes in creating and managing email marketing campaigns to promote products, services, or brand messages to a targeted audience. Their primary goal is to drive customer engagement, build brand awareness, increase website traffic, and ultimately generate leads or sales.

Key Responsibilities

Email strategy development: Creating and implementing a comprehensive email marketing strategy that aligns with the business goals, target audience, and brand voice while identifying the most suitable types of email campaigns and content for each purpose.

List management: Building and maintaining a high-quality, segmented email list by encouraging sign-ups, managing subscriptions, and ensuring compliance with data privacy regulations, such as GDPR.

Email design and content creation: Producing visually appealing and engaging email templates, as well as crafting persuasive copy tailored to the target audience, campaign objectives, and desired call-to-action.

Personalization and segmentation: Tailoring email content and targeting based on specific audience segments, demographics, or behavioral data to increase relevance, engagement, and conversion rates.

Email automation: Implementing and managing email automation tools, such as drip campaigns, triggered emails, and autoresponders, to deliver timely and relevant messages based on user behavior, preferences, or milestones.

Testing and optimization: Conducting A/B testing and multivariate testing on various email elements, such as subject lines, headlines, images, and call-to-action buttons, to identify best-performing combinations and optimize future campaigns.

Deliverability and spam management: Ensuring emails reach the intended recipients by adhering to best practices for email deliverability, maintaining a clean email list, and minimizing spam complaints.

Analytics and reporting: Tracking and analyzing email performance metrics, such as open rates, click-through rates, conversion rates, and ROI, to evaluate campaign effectiveness and adjust strategies accordingly.

AI Tools for Email Marketers

Seventh Sense is an AI-driven email marketing optimization tool that analyzes recipient engagement data to determine the best time to send emails to each subscriber, helping to maximize open and click-through rates.

Rasa.io is an AI-powered email marketing tool that automatically curates and personalizes content for subscribers based on their interests and engagement history, helping email marketers create more relevant and engaging newsletters.

Persado.com is an AI-powered content generation platform that uses natural language processing and machine learning algorithms to generate emotionally resonant and persuasive email copy, helping to improve engagement and conversion rates.

Automizy is an email marketing automation tool that incorporates AI algorithms to optimize subject lines, send times, and automation workflows, helping email marketers improve their campaign performance.

Affiliate Marketers

An affiliate marketer promotes products or services offered by a company or a merchant and earns a commission for each sale or lead generated through their marketing efforts. Their primary goal is to drive traffic, generate leads, and increase sales for the merchant by leveraging various online marketing channels, strategies, and tactics.

Key Responsibilities

Niche selection: Identifying a profitable niche or market segment in which they have an interest or expertise, and selecting relevant products or services to promote.

Affiliate program research: Finding and joining suitable affiliate programs or networks that offer the chosen products or services and provide attractive commission structures and support.

Content creation: Producing high-quality, engaging, and informative content in various formats (e.g., blog posts, articles, videos, podcasts, or social media updates) to attract and educate the target audience about the products or services being promoted.

Product or service promotion: Strategically promoting the chosen products or services within their content or through dedicated promotional campaigns, using techniques such as product reviews, comparisons, tutorials, or case studies, and including unique affiliate links or tracking codes.

Traffic generation: Driving targeted traffic to their content or promotional materials using various online marketing channels and tactics, such as search engine optimization (SEO), pay-per-click (PPC) advertising, social media marketing, email marketing, or content marketing.

Conversion optimization: Implementing and testing strategies to increase the conversion rate of their marketing efforts, such as optimizing landing pages, using persuasive copy, or employing effective calls-to-action.

Relationship management: Building and maintaining relationships with affiliate program managers or merchants to negotiate better commission rates, request promotional materials or exclusive offers, and stay informed about product updates or policy changes.

Tracking and analytics: Monitoring and analyzing performance metrics, such as traffic, conversions, commissions, and return on investment (ROI), to evaluate the effectiveness of their marketing efforts, identify areas for improvement, and adjust strategies accordingly.

AI Tools for Affiliate Marketers

There aren't specific AI tools for affiliate marketers. Instead, they use many of the same tools as other digital marketers and content creators because their key responsibilities.

Spotlight: GetResponse

GetResponse   Product ›   Pricing   Resources ›   Q

Marketing
beyond email

Image credit: GetResponse

GetResponse is an all-in-one online marketing platform designed to help businesses grow through various digital marketing channels. It provides tools and features for email marketing, marketing automation, landing page creation, webinars, and more.

Key Features

Email Marketing: GetResponse offers tools for creating, sending, and managing professional-looking email campaigns, including a drag-and-drop email editor, responsive email templates, and advanced personalization options.

Marketing Automation: With GetResponse, you can create automated workflows based on user behavior, segmenting your audience and sending targeted messages at the right time. This helps improve engagement, lead nurturing, and conversion rates.

Landing Pages: GetResponse includes a drag-and-drop landing page builder that allows you to create visually appealing and high-converting landing pages without coding or design skills.

Webinars: GetResponse offers a built-in webinar platform that enables you to host live webinars, on-demand webinars, or video meetings, making it easier to connect with your audience and generate leads.

Funnels: The platform features a conversion funnel builder that helps you create and optimize sales, lead generation, or webinar funnels, guiding your audience through each step of the conversion process.

Forms and Surveys: GetResponse provides a variety of customizable forms and surveys to help you collect valuable information about your audience, segment them based on their preferences, and tailor your marketing campaigns accordingly.

Analytics and Reporting: GetResponse offers in-depth analytics and reporting features that help you track and analyze the performance of your marketing campaigns, providing insights into opens, clicks, conversions, and more.

Integrations: GetResponse integrates with various third-party tools and services, such as e-commerce platforms, CRM systems, and social media networks, enabling you to connect and synchronize your marketing efforts across different channels.

AI Tools

GetResponse is one of the most innovative digital market apps with AI capabilities for building websites, recommending products, and generating email subject lines.

Spotlight: Semrush

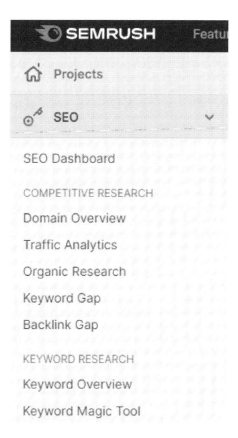

Image credit: Semrush

Semrush is a comprehensive digital marketing and search engine optimization (SEO) tool that helps businesses improve their online visibility, drive more traffic, and increase sales. It provides a range of features and data insights, covering areas such as SEO, paid advertising, content marketing, social media marketing, and competitive analysis.

Key Features

- Semrush provides extensive keyword research capabilities, helping you find the most relevant and profitable keywords for your business. In addition, it offers data on search volume, keyword difficulty, cost-per-click (CPC), and more.
- Semrush's site audit feature helps you identify and fix on-page and technical SEO issues on your website, ensuring optimal performance and search engine visibility.
- Semrush lets you analyze your website's backlink profile and identify valuable link-building opportunities. It also helps you monitor and disavow potentially harmful or low-quality backlinks.
- With Semrush, you can track your website's search engine rankings for specific keywords, allowing you to measure your SEO performance over time and adjust your strategies accordingly.
- Semrush allows you to monitor and analyze your competitors' online marketing strategies, including their organic search rankings, paid advertising campaigns, and content marketing efforts. This helps you identify gaps, opportunities, and best practices to improve your marketing efforts.
- Semrush provides insights into your competitors' paid advertising strategies, such as their ad creatives, keywords, and ad spending. This information can help you optimize your pay-per-click (PPC) campaigns for better ROI.

- Semrush offers a suite of tools for creating, optimizing, and promoting content. These include a content audit tool and content planner.
- Semrush includes social media management and analytics tools that help you schedule, monitor, and analyze your marketing efforts across various platforms.
- Semrush's traffic analytics feature provides insights into your website's traffic sources, visitor behavior, and engagement metrics, enabling you to make data-driven decisions about your marketing strategies.
- Semrush integrates with various third-party tools and platforms, such as Google Analytics, Google Search Console, and Google Data Studio, allowing you to consolidate and analyze data from multiple sources.

AI Tool

The SEO Writing Assistant (SWA) allows writers to optimize their content based on their targeted keywords and results from search engines.

7. MAKE MONEY ONLINE FREELANCING

The freelance market, side hustle, and gig economy have experienced remarkable growth and diversification in recent years. With the increasing adoption of remote work and digital tools, more people than ever are exploring alternative ways to earn income and achieve a more outstanding work-life balance.

The rise of online platforms has made it easier for workers to connect with clients and pursue opportunities across various industries. From software development to content creation, the gig economy has evolved to offer a wide range of professional services.

As the landscape continues to shift, governments worldwide are working to develop regulations that protect gig workers' rights and ensure fair labor practices. In an era marked by economic uncertainty and changing employment dynamics, the freelance market, side hustle, and gig economy have emerged as critical components of the global workforce.

Freelancers

Freelancers are self-employed individuals who provide client services project-by-project or contractually. They typically work independently and have the flexibility to choose their clients, set their schedules, and negotiate their payment rates. Freelancers can be found in a variety of industries.

Freelancers generally handle all aspects of their business, such as finding clients, marketing their services, managing contracts, invoicing, and tax reporting. The benefits of freelancing include flexibility, independence, and the opportunity to work in various industries or projects. However, freelancers also face challenges, such as inconsistent income, lack of benefits, and the need to find new clients to maintain a steady workload.

Getting Started - All Freelancers

First, building a successful freelancing career takes time, persistence, and patience. Secondly, you should focus on providing excellent service, maintaining strong client relationships, and consistently delivering quality work to grow your reputation and client base. For example, Fiverr and Udemy showcase customer reviews for freelancers to help potential buyers select freelancers for their projects.

Here are some steps to help you launch your freelancing career:

Assess your skills and interests: Identify your strengths, expertise, and the services you want to offer as a freelancer. Consider any relevant experience, education, or certifications you have in your chosen field.

Create a portfolio: Showcase your work and demonstrate your skills to potential clients. Your portfolio could include samples of your writing, design work, code, or other relevant projects. You can create a website or use online portfolio platforms like Behance, Dribbble, or GitHub, depending on your field.

Set your rates: Research the market rates for your services, considering your experience, expertise, and the value you provide. You can charge hourly, per project, or on a retainer basis.

Develop a professional online presence: Create a LinkedIn profile, personal website, or social media account dedicated to your freelancing business. This will help potential clients find you and learn more about your services.

Network: Connect with other professionals in your industry, and attend conferences, workshops, or online events. Join online communities and forums related to your niche.

Networking can help you find clients, learn from others, and stay informed about industry trends.

Find clients: Start by contacting your existing network, such as friends, family, and former colleagues. You can also use freelancing platforms like Fiverr, Upwork, or Freelancer to find projects. Additionally, explore job boards, social media, and professional networks to find potential clients.

Pitch your services: Craft a compelling pitch that highlights your expertise, experience, and the value you provide. Then, tailor your pitch to each potential client, addressing their needs and how your services can help them.

Set up a business structure: Depending on your location and the nature of your freelancing work, you may need to register as a sole proprietor, create a limited liability company (LLC), or establish another business structure.

Manage finances: Open a separate bank account for your freelancing business, track your income and expenses, and set aside money for taxes. Consider using accounting software or working with a professional to help manage your finances.

Create contracts and invoices: Use clear contracts to outline project terms, scope, payment details, and deadlines. Send professional invoices to clients, including a description of your services, payment terms, and contact information.

Image credit: Fiverr

Making Money - All Freelancers

Freelancers often employ various strategies to maximize their earnings, such as diversifying their client base, offering multiple services, and continually refining their skills to stay competitive. In addition, they typically set their rates based on their experience, expertise, and market demand. Here are some ways freelancers can earn money:

- Hourly rates: Some freelancers charge clients an hourly rate for their work. They track their time on a project and bill the client accordingly.
- Fixed-price projects: Freelancers may agree on a fixed price for a specific project, which is determined upfront. The payment could be made upon project completion or split into milestones.
- Retainer agreements: In a retainer agreement, freelancers receive a recurring fee for ongoing services or access to their expertise over a specified period. This can provide a more stable income stream.
- Value-based pricing: Some freelancers charge based on the value they bring to the client's business rather than the time they spend on the project. This pricing model requires a deep understanding of the client's needs and the potential return on investment.
- Royalties or revenue sharing: In some cases, freelancers may negotiate royalties or a revenue-sharing agreement, earning a percentage of sales or profit generated by their work.
- Additional services: Freelancers can offer add-on services, such as consulting, training, or maintenance, to supplement their income.
- Digital products: Freelancers can create digital products like e-books, online courses, or templates related to their expertise and sell them online.
- Passive income streams: Some freelancers build passive income streams, such as affiliate marketing, advertising revenue from a blog, or licensing their work.

Popular Freelancer Professions

Let's review several in-demand freelancer professions, how ChatGPT can help, and AI tools for business growth.

Graphic Designers

Graphic designers create visual concepts and designs to communicate ideas, convey messages, or represent brand identity. They use a combination of typography, images, illustrations, colors, and layout techniques to produce visually appealing and effective designs.

Graphic designers should have a strong foundation in design principles, creativity, attention to detail, and proficiency in design software, such as Adobe Creative Suite (Illustrator, Photoshop, InDesign) or other similar tools. They also need strong communication and interpersonal skills to collaborate with clients and team members effectively.

Key Duties

- Understanding client needs, objectives, and target audience
- Developing design concepts, either independently or as part of a team
- Producing drafts, sketches, or prototypes for client review
- Refining designs based on feedback and making necessary revisions
- Collaborating with other professionals, such as copywriters, developers, or marketing specialists
- Ensuring design consistency and adhering to brand guidelines

Graphic designers work on a variety of projects across different mediums, such as:

Branding and logo design: Creating unique logos, visual identities, and brand guidelines for businesses or organizations.

Print materials: Designing items such as brochures, flyers, posters, business cards, packaging, and print advertisements.

Digital design: Creating web graphics, social media visuals, email templates, and digital advertisements.

Web design: Designing the visual appearance and layout of websites, including graphics, colors, fonts, and navigation elements.

User interface (UI) design: Crafting the visual elements and layouts of software applications, mobile apps, or other digital products to enhance user experience.

Infographics: Designing visual representations of data or information to make it easily digestible and engaging for the audience.

Illustration: Creating custom artwork or illustrations for various design projects.

Motion graphics and animation: Designing visual elements and animations for video content, presentations, or interactive media.

Using ChatGPT

While ChatGPT cannot directly create visual designs, it can still assist graphic designers in various ways during their creative process and day-to-day tasks. Here are some ways ChatGPT can help graphic designers:

ChatGPT can help generate design concepts or ideas based on specific project requirements or client needs, which can be a useful starting point for graphic designers.

ChatGPT can provide suggestions on color schemes, typography, or layout styles to help graphic designers explore different design approaches.

ChatGPT can help generate text content for design projects, such as headlines, taglines, or call-to-action phrases, making it easier for graphic designers to focus on the visual aspects.

ChatGPT can assist in creating or refining design briefs, ensuring clear communication of project objectives, requirements, and expectations.

ChatGPT can help draft emails or project proposals to clients, making it easier for graphic designers to communicate their ideas, project updates, or other relevant information professionally.

ChatGPT can assist in creating engaging descriptions for design projects in a portfolio, helping designers showcase their work effectively.

Prompt Examples

- "Create the requirements for a client who wants me to design a marketing pamphlet."
- "What are some tagline ideas for a new perfume that smells like oak?"
- "Draft an email for a client who has exceeded her project budget."
- "What design elements should I include for a car company logo?"
- "Provide a color scheme for an electrical parts website."

AI Tools for Graphic Designers

Image credit: Adobe

Adobe Sensei: Adobe's AI and machine learning framework are integrated into various Adobe Creative Cloud applications, such as Photoshop, Illustrator, and InDesign. It helps with content-aware features, automated image manipulation, and design asset recommendations.

RunwayML is a platform that allows graphic designers to utilize machine learning models for image and video editing. It offers features such as image synthesis, style transfer, and object removal.

Created by OpenAI, DALL-E is an AI tool that generates images from textual descriptions. Although not publicly available, the technology shows promise for graphic designers in creating visual concepts based on textual input.

Remove.bg: This AI-powered tool automatically removes image backgrounds, making it easier for graphic designers to isolate subjects and create composite images.

LetsEnhance.io is an AI-driven image upscaling and enhancement tool that helps improve image resolution and quality without compromising detail or introducing artifacts.

Looka uses AI to generate logo ideas based on user preferences, making it easier for graphic designers to create unique and personalized logo concepts.

ColorMind.io is an AI-powered color palette generator that suggests harmonious color combinations for graphic design projects.

Spotlight: Canva

Image credit: Canva

Canva is an online graphic design platform that allows users to create various types of visual content easily and quickly. It is designed for professionals and non-designers.

Canva offers a user-friendly interface and a wide range of customizable templates for various design projects, such as social media posts, presentations, posters, infographics, logos, and more.

Key Features

Drag-and-drop editor: Canva's intuitive interface makes it easy for users to create designs by dragging and dropping elements, resizing images, and editing text.

Templates: Canva offers a vast library of professionally-designed templates for different purposes, which users can customize according to their needs and preferences.

Design elements: Canva provides a wide selection of design elements, such as images, illustrations, icons, shapes, and fonts, allowing users to create visually appealing and unique designs.

Image editing: Canva includes essential editing tools, such as cropping, resizing, filters, and adjustments, allowing users to enhance their images directly within the platform.

Collaboration: Canva supports real-time collaboration, enabling multiple users to work on a design simultaneously and share their work with others.

Cloud storage: Canva saves designs in the cloud, allowing users to access and edit their work from any device with an internet connection.

Export options: Canva lets users download their designs in various file formats, such as JPG, PNG, PDF, or GIF, and also supports direct sharing to social media platforms or embedding on websites.

AI Tools

Magic Write in Canva Docs is an AI text generator to help you produce a first draft fast. Start with a prompt and watch as copy, blog outlines, lists, bio captions, content ideas, brainstorms, and more appear in seconds.

Canva's AI image generator creates images that visualize a product or idea, sketch out a creative concept, or push the limits of what's possible. For example, type your text prompt: "A lion driving a car through a city." Next, watch your words and phrases transform into beautiful images you can use for your projects.

Social Media Managers

Social media managers plan, implement, and manage an organization's or individual's social media presence and strategy. Their goals are to increase brand awareness, build an engaged online community, and support marketing and communication objectives through various social media platforms, such as Facebook, Instagram, Twitter, LinkedIn, Pinterest, and others.

Key Duties

Content creation and curation: Social media managers develop and curate content, such as images, videos, articles, and graphics, that is relevant, engaging, and consistent with the organization's brand and messaging.

Content scheduling and posting: They plan and schedule content to be published on various social media platforms, ensuring a consistent posting frequency and timing to maximize reach and engagement.

Social media strategy development: Social media managers create and execute social media strategies that align with the organization's goals, target audience, and overall marketing plan.

Community management: They monitor and engage with the online community, responding to comments, questions, and messages from followers, fostering positive relationships, and maintaining a strong brand presence.

Analytics and reporting: Social media managers track and analyze social media performance data to determine the effectiveness of their campaigns and strategies, making adjustments as needed to optimize results. They often create and present reports to showcase these insights.

Advertising and promotions: They plan, create, and manage social media advertising campaigns, targeting specific audiences to increase brand visibility, generate leads, or drive sales.

Crisis management: Social media managers monitor online conversations and sentiments around the brand, addressing any negative comments or potential crises that may arise and working to maintain a positive brand image.

Influencer partnerships and collaborations: They identify, reach out to, and collaborate with influencers or brand ambassadors to increase brand visibility and reach new audiences.

Watch trends: Like all marketers, social media managers keep abreast of the latest social media trends, tools, and best practices, adapting their strategies to stay relevant and effective in the ever-changing digital landscape.

Cross-functional collaboration: They often work closely with other departments, such as marketing, public relations, sales, and customer service, ensuring that social media efforts are aligned with broader organizational objectives.

Using ChatGPT

Here are some ways ChatGPT can help social media managers:

Content creation—ChatGPT can help generate ideas, captions, or even complete social media posts, assisting social media managers in creating engaging and relevant content for their target audience.

Content curation—ChatGPT can provide suggestions for articles, links, or resources relevant to a specific topic, helping social media managers curate high-quality content to share with their audience.

Trend analysis—ChatGPT can be used to gather information about the latest social media trends, tools, and best practices, allowing social media managers to stay up-to-date and adapt their strategies accordingly.

Hashtag suggestions—ChatGPT can help generate hashtag ideas for social media posts, helping social media managers increase the visibility and reach of their content.

Community engagement—ChatGPT can help draft responses to comments, questions, or messages from followers, assisting social media managers in maintaining a consistent and engaging brand presence.

Analytics and reporting—ChatGPT can help summarize performance data or create reports, providing insights into the effectiveness of social media campaigns and strategies.

Creative brainstorming—ChatGPT can be used to generate ideas for social media campaigns, promotions, or content themes.

Influencer research—ChatGPT can provide information about potential influencers or brand ambassadors in a specific niche or industry, helping social media managers identify collaboration opportunities.

Prompt Examples

- "Generate five ideas for Facebook posts about suntan lotion for millennials. Include CTA, images, and hashtags wherever possible."
- "List ten hashtags for my fashion contest on Instagram."
- "Provide five quotes from American business leaders to post on Twitter."
- "Write an interesting and engaging question to post on my Facebook Group about dreaming."
- "Draft three brief responses to LinkedIn users who ask me for more info about my small business consulting services. Include call-to-actions for all of them."

AI Tools for Social Media Managers

In addition to Buffer, Hootsuite, Sprout Social, and BuzzSumo; here are some of the best AI tools for social media managers.

Brand24 is a social media monitoring and analytics tool that tracks mentions, sentiment, and engagement across various platforms. It helps social media marketers monitor their brand reputation, respond to customer feedback, and discover influencers in their industry.

SocialPilot is a social media management tool offering features like scheduling, analytics, and advertising management. It also provides collaboration tools for team members and client management.

Loomly is a social media calendar and management tool that uses AI to provide content ideas, optimize post timing, and offer audience insights. It also supports collaboration and provides analytics.

RiteTag is a hashtag optimization tool that uses AI to recommend the most relevant and effective hashtags for social media posts, helping increase visibility and engagement.

Voice-Over Artists

Voice-over artists provide vocal performances for various types of media projects, using their voices to convey information, emotions, or characters. They typically work in recording studios, using high-quality microphones and audio equipment to create clear and compelling voice recordings. Voice-over artists lend their talents to a wide range of projects, including:

- Commercials: Voice-over artists record promotional messages for radio, television, or online advertisements, helping brands effectively communicate their products or services.
- Animation and video games: They provide voices for characters in animated films, television shows, or video games, bringing life and personality to the characters through their vocal performances.
- Narration: Voice-over artists narrate documentaries, audiobooks, e-learning materials, or instructional videos, using their voices to guide the audience through the content and convey information clearly and engagingly.
- Radio and podcasts: They may work as announcers or hosts for radio shows or podcasts, providing introductions, transitions, or commentary.
- Voice assistants and AI: Voice-over artists record the voices used in virtual assistants, chatbots, or other AI applications, making these technologies more engaging and human-like.
- IVR (Interactive Voice Response) systems: They record the voice prompts and messages used in telephone systems, such as customer service lines or automated call menus.
- Dubbing and localization: Voice-over artists record dialogues for foreign films, television shows, or video games, translating and adapting the content to the local language and culture.

Using ChatGPT

Here are some ways ChatGPT can assist voice-over artists:

Script analysis: ChatGPT can help voice-over artists understand and break down a script, offering insights into the context, emotions, or characters involved, which can inform their vocal performance.

Pronunciation guidance: ChatGPT can provide pronunciation tips or phonetic spellings for unfamiliar words, names, or technical terms, ensuring clarity and accuracy in the voice-over artist's performance.

Character development: ChatGPT can help voice-over artists brainstorm character traits, backgrounds, or vocal qualities, allowing them to create unique and engaging voices for their projects.

Accent and dialect coaching: ChatGPT can provide information and guidance on different accents and dialects, assisting voice-over artists in expanding their range and versatility.

Audition preparation: ChatGPT can help voice-over artists prepare for auditions by suggesting performance tips, offering feedback on their delivery, or helping them create a compelling character backstory.

Copywriting and script editing: ChatGPT can assist in writing or editing scripts for voice-over projects, ensuring that the text is clear, engaging, and well-suited for vocal performance.

Prompt Examples

- "What are the main differences between Irish and English accents?"
- "Give me some ideas for character traits for an 8-foot ogre."
- "Discuss the various types of voice-over projects you have worked on, from commercials to audiobooks, and share your favorite experiences or unique challenges you faced."

119

- "How do you create distinct character voices and maintain consistency across different recording sessions, especially when working on animation or video games?"
- "Share your advice for aspiring voice-over artists, including essential skills, tools, and resources they should be aware of as they begin their careers in the industry."

AI Tools for Voice Over Artists

There's a new way to make video and podcasts. A good way.

Descript is the simple, powerful, and fun way to edit.

Get started for free →   See product tour

Image credit: Descript

Descript is an audio and video editing software that uses AI to transcribe and edit recordings. It's a valuable tool for voice-over artists looking to create, edit, or fine-tune their recordings quickly and efficiently.

Adobe Audition is a professional audio editing software that offers AI-powered features, such as automatic speech alignment, noise reduction, and adaptive noise cancellation, helping voice-over artists improve the quality of their recordings.

Auphonic is an AI-based audio processing tool that automatically adjusts the levels, noise, and overall quality of voice recordings, making it easier for voice-over artists to achieve a polished and professional sound.

Voice-booking.com helps create synthesized voice-overs using AI-generated voices, which can be helpful for voice-over artists in creating temporary voice tracks for projects or experimenting with different vocal styles.

izotope RX is an audio repair and editing software that uses AI algorithms to remove noise, clicks, and other audio issues from voice recordings, helping voice-over artists achieve a professional sound.

Murf.ai creates realistic text-to-voice across 20 Languages and 130+ natural AI voices.

Brain.fm is an AI-generated music platform that creates focus-enhancing soundscapes, which can help voice-over artists maintain concentration and creativity during their work sessions.

Audio Creators

Audio creators produce, record, and edit audio content for various media and entertainment projects. For example, they may be or work with voice actors, musicians, or sound effects to create an immersive and engaging audio experience for the audience. Audio creators can work in several industries, such as music production, radio, podcasts, film, television, video games, advertising, and more.

Key Duties

Recording: Audio creators capture high-quality recordings of voices, instruments, sound effects, or other audio elements using microphones, audio interfaces, and recording software.

Editing: They edit and arrange the recorded audio, removing unwanted noises, adjusting timing, and fine-tuning the overall sound to create a polished and professional final product.

Mixing: Audio creators mix different audio elements, such as dialogue, music, and sound effects, balancing their levels, panning, and applying equalization, compression, or other audio processing techniques to achieve a cohesive and engaging sound.

Sound design: In some cases, audio creators may be responsible for sound design, which involves creating unique and realistic sound effects or ambient sounds to enhance a project's overall atmosphere and storytelling.

Music production: Audio creators working in music production may compose, arrange, or produce original music, working with musicians or using virtual instruments and software to create the desired sound.

Foley and ADR (Automated Dialogue Replacement): Audio creators working in film or television may record and edit Foley sounds (custom sound effects recorded in sync with the visuals) or ADR, replacing original on-set dialogue with cleaner, studio-recorded dialogue.

Podcast production: Audio creators working on podcasts may be responsible for recording interviews or narration, editing content, adding music or sound effects, and ensuring consistent sound quality across episodes.

Audio restoration: Audio creators may also work on restoring damaged or low-quality audio recordings, using specialized tools and techniques to remove noise, clicks, or other imperfections.

Live sound engineering: Some audio creators may work in live sound, setting up and managing audio equipment for concerts, theater productions, or other live events, ensuring optimal sound quality and balance for the audience.

Using ChatGPT

Here are some ways ChatGPT can help audio creators:

Idea generation: ChatGPT can help audio creators brainstorm ideas for sound design, music composition, or podcast topics, providing inspiration and sparking creativity.

Technical guidance: ChatGPT can provide information on audio equipment, software, or techniques, helping audio creators make informed decisions and expand their technical knowledge.

Troubleshooting: ChatGPT can help audio creators with problem-solving when they encounter challenges or issues with their audio projects, offering suggestions and solutions to overcome obstacles.

Content creation: ChatGPT can assist in writing scripts, articles, or blog posts related to audio production, sound design, or other relevant topics, allowing audio creators to share their expertise and build their online presence.

Prompt Examples

- "What are the most popular ways to filter our background noise for an audio track?"
- "Share the process of creating an immersive audio experience: How do you approach sound design, music

selection, and balancing various audio elements to tell a compelling story?"
- "Discuss your approach to collaborating with other audio creators, such as voice-over artists, musicians, or sound engineers, to produce high-quality audio content."
- "What are some ways to overcome creative blocks as an audio creator?
- "Write a 10 to 20-word jingle for a pumpkin soup."

AI Tools for Audio Creators

Audacity is a popular, open-source audio editing software that features AI-based noise reduction and audio enhancement tools, making it an excellent option for voice-over artists to polish their recordings.

Landr is an AI-powered platform for music mastering, offering automated mastering services that analyze and optimize audio tracks for professional sound quality.

Sonix is an AI-powered transcription service that can automatically transcribe audio recordings into text, which can help audio creators with projects requiring written scripts, captions, or documentation.

Spleeter is an AI-powered source separation tool that can isolate individual elements (vocals, drums, bass, etc.) from a mixed audio track, allowing audio creators to remix, sample, or manipulate existing music.

Magenta by Google is a research project by Google that explores AI-generated music and art, offering various tools and resources for audio creators to experiment with AI-assisted composition and sound design.

Photographers

Photographers use their artistic and technical skills to capture images using cameras. Their work involves composing, framing, and taking photographs that tell a story, convey a message, or evoke an emotion. Photographers can specialize in various fields or genres, and their responsibilities may vary accordingly.

Photographers must have a strong understanding of camera equipment, lighting, composition, and editing techniques. They should also possess creativity, patience, attention to detail, and strong communication skills to work effectively with clients and subjects.

Some of the most common types of photographers include:

Portrait photographers: They take pictures of individuals or groups, capturing their subjects' personalities, emotions, or expressions. Portrait photographers may work with families, couples, children, or professionals seeking headshots.

Wedding photographers: They specialize in photographing weddings, capturing the ceremony, reception, and other special moments throughout the event. Wedding photographers often work closely with clients to understand their preferences and style.

Commercial photographers: They create images for advertising, marketing, or promotional purposes, working with clients to showcase products, services, or brands. Depending on the client's needs, commercial photographers may take photos of food, fashion, products, architecture, or other subjects.

Fine art photographers create images meant to be displayed in galleries, museums, or private collections. Fine art photographers often have a unique style or perspective and may focus on specific subjects, themes, or techniques.

Photojournalists: They capture images that document news events, people, or places for newspapers, magazines, or online publications. Photojournalists often work in fast-paced environments and must be able to adapt to changing situations and conditions.

Sports photographers specialize in capturing images of athletes, competitions, or sporting events. Therefore, sports photographers must be skilled at capturing fast-moving subjects and anticipating the best moments to take a photo.

Wildlife and nature photographers: They focus on capturing images of animals, plants, landscapes, or other natural subjects. Wildlife and nature photographers often spend time outdoors, traveling to remote locations to grab unique and compelling images.

Event photographers: They are hired to document special events, such as conferences, parties, or performances, capturing the atmosphere, guests, and critical moments.

Using ChatGPT

ChatGPT can be a valuable resource for photographers, assisting them in various aspects of their work and supporting their creative and business processes.

Idea generation: ChatGPT can help photographers brainstorm ideas for photo projects, compositions, or concepts, inspiring and sparking creativity.

Technical guidance: ChatGPT can provide information on camera equipment, photography techniques, or editing tools, helping photographers make informed decisions and expand their technical knowledge.

Troubleshooting: ChatGPT can help photographers with problem-solving when they encounter challenges or issues with their photography projects, offering suggestions and solutions to overcome obstacles.

Prompt Examples

- "What are five things I should consider for nightlife photography?"

- "Share your top tips for capturing stunning landscape photographs, including camera settings, composition techniques, and lighting considerations."
- "Discuss your approach to post-processing: What are your favorite editing tools and techniques to enhance your images?"
- "How do you build rapport with clients during portrait sessions and capture their personalities while making them feel comfortable and relaxed in front of the camera?"
- "What filters do you recommend for a classic or vintage feel?"

AI Tools for Photographers

Image credit: Pixlr

Pixlr is a free online photo editor that includes AI-powered features, such as background removal and automatic photo enhancement, helping photographers make quick edits and adjustments to their images.

Adobe Photoshop and Lightroom—Adobe's popular image editing software incorporates AI-powered features, such as Select Subject, Content-Aware Fill, and Enhance Details, which can help photographers edit and retouch their images more efficiently.

Luminar Neo and Luminar AI are AI-powered photo editing software offering various automated tools, such as Sky Replacement, Portrait Enhancer, and Structure AI, making it easier for photographers to achieve professional results quickly.

Topaz Labs offers a suite of AI-based tools for photographers, including Topaz Gigapixel AI (for upscaling images), Topaz Sharpen AI (for enhancing sharpness), and Topaz DeNoise AI (for reducing noise in photos).

ON1 Photo RAW is an all-in-one photo organizer, editor, and effects app that incorporates AI-powered features like Sky Swap AI, NoNoise AI, and Portrait AI, helping photographers achieve better results in their editing process.

Skylum AirMagic is an AI-powered photo editing tool specifically designed for drone and aerial photography, automatically enhancing images by adjusting brightness, contrast, sharpness, and other parameters.

NeuralStyler.com is an AI-based application that transforms images, videos, and GIFs into artistic creations using neural networks, offering photographers an innovative way to experiment with styles and visual effects.

Videographers

Videographers specialize in capturing, editing, and producing video content. They use their artistic and technical skills to create visual stories, convey messages, or evoke emotions through moving images. Videographers can work across various industries and may focus on different types of projects, such as:

- Event videography: Videographers in this field capture special events like weddings, parties, conferences, or performances, documenting the atmosphere, guests, and critical moments.
- Corporate videography: Corporate videographers create video content for businesses and organizations, producing promotional videos, training materials, product demonstrations, or internal communications.
- Documentary filmmaking: Documentary videographers tell stories about real-life events, people, or issues through their video work. They may focus on social, cultural, political, or environmental topics and often aim to inform or raise awareness about their subjects.
- Commercial videography: Commercial videographers produce video content for advertising or marketing purposes, working with clients to showcase products, services, or brands. This may involve creating commercials, branded content, or social media videos.
- Music video production: Music video videographers collaborate with musicians or bands to create visually compelling videos that complement songs or albums. They may be involved in the creative direction, planning, shooting, and editing of music videos.
- Sports videography: Sports videographers capture footage of athletes, competitions, or sporting events, often working in fast-paced environments to document the action and excitement of the games.

- Real estate videography: Real estate videographers create video tours or promotional materials for residential or commercial properties, showcasing their features and helping potential buyers visualize the spaces.

Using ChatGPT

Technical guidance: ChatGPT can provide information on camera equipment, video production techniques, or editing tools, helping videographers make informed decisions and expand their technical knowledge.

Troubleshooting: ChatGPT can help videographers problem-solve when they encounter challenges or issues with their video projects, offering suggestions and solutions to overcome obstacles.

Idea generation: ChatGPT can help videographers brainstorm ideas for video projects, storylines, or shot compositions.

Content creation: ChatGPT can assist in writing articles, blog posts, or social media content related to videography, allowing videographers to share their expertise and build their online presence.

Prompt Examples

- "Discuss your approach to color grading and post-production: What are your favorite apps and techniques for enhancing your videos and creating a consistent visual style?"
- "How do you plan and execute a successful video shoot, from pre-production and storyboarding to directing talent and managing unexpected events on set?"
- "What suggestions do you have for videographers looking to create engaging storytelling through visual and audio elements in their video projects?"

- "What are some storyline ideas for rebuilding a 100-year-old church by residents?"
- "Provide a list of top-rated handheld video recorders from the 1990s to use in a film about NYC during that decade."

AI Tools for Videographers

Adobe Premiere Pro—Adobe's popular video editing software incorporates AI-powered features, such as Auto Reframe, Content-Aware Fill, and Color Match, which can help videographers edit and enhance their videos more efficiently.

Final Cut Pro X is a professional video editing software for Mac that includes AI-powered features like Smart Conform, which automatically resizes videos to fit different aspect ratios.

Filmstro is a music scoring software that uses AI to analyze video footage and suggest suitable music tracks based on the mood and tone of the scenes.

Animoto is an AI-powered video creation platform that offers various automated tools and templates, making it easier for videographers to create professional-looking videos quickly.

Wipster is a video review and approval platform incorporating AI-powered features like automated feedback, which analyzes videos and provides suggested improvements or corrections.

Magisto is an AI-powered video editor that automatically transforms raw footage into polished videos with pre-designed styles and templates.

Veed.io is a web-based video editing tool that offers AI-powered features like automated subtitles and voiceovers, which can help videographers save time and effort.

Motion AI is an AI-based platform that allows videographers to create animated graphics and visual effects using machine learning algorithms.

Nvidia Maxine is a cloud-based platform that offers AI-powered video conferencing features, such as noise cancellation, virtual backgrounds, and facial animation, enhancing the quality and experience of remote meetings and interviews.

Doodly is an AI-assisted whiteboard animation software that allows users to create explainer videos by simply dragging and dropping elements onto the canvas.

Synthesia.io is the website and platform for Synthesia, a company specializing in AI-driven video synthesis technology. The platform uses artificial intelligence and deep learning algorithms to generate realistic videos with computer-generated characters, commonly called "deep fakes."

Consultants

Consultants provide expert advice and recommendations to businesses or organizations in specific areas of expertise. Consultants work with clients to identify problems, opportunities, or challenges and provide solutions or strategies to address them. They may work independently, as part of a consulting firm, or in-house for a company. Some common areas of consultancy include:

Management: Management consultants advise on strategic planning, organizational structure, process improvement, and performance optimization to help businesses achieve their goals and improve their operations.

IT: IT consultants advise businesses on technology solutions, such as software development, network infrastructure, cybersecurity, or data management, to improve efficiency, productivity, and security.

Marketing: Marketing consultants provide advice on marketing strategy, brand positioning, customer segmentation, and digital marketing tactics to help businesses reach their target audience and achieve their marketing objectives.

Human Resources: Human resources consultants advise on recruitment, talent management, employee engagement, and workplace culture to help businesses attract and retain top talent and improve their overall performance.

Finance: Finance consultants advise businesses on financial management, such as budgeting, forecasting, risk management, and investment strategies, to help them make informed financial decisions and achieve their financial objectives.

Legal: Legal consultants advise businesses on legal issues, such as contracts, regulations, intellectual property, and litigation, to help companies to navigate legal challenges and comply with the law.

Using ChatGPT

ChatGPT can be a valuable consultant resource, providing insights, information, and tools to enhance their work and deliver better client results. For instance, it can help consultants with idea generation, research, analysis, technical guidance, communication, presentation, marketing, and program management in their respective fields.

Prompt Examples

- "Write a brief introduction for a speech I'm giving about chatbots."
- "Create a PowerPoint presentation with the following text: [Text]."
- "Write a thank you email for a client, including a request to have a second meeting."
- "Act as a marketing consultant. Provide a list of the seven best apps to manage online ads."
- "What skills do consultants need to be successful?"

AI Tools for Consultants

AI tools for consultants vary depending on their field of expertise. So, review relevant job profiles in this book and search "ai tools for (*your profession*) consultants" for the most current apps, for example, ai tools for small business consultants.

Translators

Translators convert written or spoken content from one language to another while preserving the original meaning, tone, and style. Translators work across various industries and may translate a wide range of materials, such as:

Literary works—Translators specialize in translating books, poetry, or other creative pieces from one language to another, making them accessible to readers in different countries.

Legal documents—Legal translators specialize in translating legal documents, such as contracts, patents, or court documents, ensuring accuracy and compliance with legal terminology and standards.

Medical documents—Medical translators specialize in translating medical records, such as clinical trial reports, medical histories, or patient information leaflets, requiring a deep understanding of medical terminology and concepts.

Technical documents—Technical translators specialize in translating technical documents, such as user manuals, software documentation, or engineering reports, requiring expertise in technical terminology and concepts.

Business documents—Business translators specialize in translating business documents, such as financial reports, marketing materials, or employee handbooks, requiring a deep understanding of business terminology and communication styles.

Website content—Website translators specialize in translating website content, such as product descriptions, customer reviews, or user interfaces, ensuring that the translated content is culturally appropriate and easy to understand.

Using ChatGPT

Draft translations: ChatGPT can provide quick text translations from one language to another. While the translations might not always be perfect, they can serve as a starting point or draft for professional translators to review, edit, and refine.

Language reference: Translators can use ChatGPT to look up vocabulary, idiomatic expressions, or grammar rules in the source or target language, helping them ensure accurate translations.

Contextual understanding: If a translator encounters an unclear or ambiguous phrase in the source text, ChatGPT can help provide context or additional information to clarify the meaning, assisting the translator in making informed decisions about the most accurate translation.

Proofreading assistance: Translators can use ChatGPT to review their translations and detect any errors, inconsistencies, or awkward phrasings that might need revision.

Cultural insights: ChatGPT can provide cultural context, background information, or relevant historical details that may help translators better understand the nuances of the source text and produce translations that resonate with the target audience.

Prompt Examples

- "What are the main differences between Mexican and Colombian Spanish?"
- "Translate the following text from English to German."
- "Review the following text for errors."
- "What grammar rules apply to the French language regarding gender?"
- "What are some cultural differences between northern and southern Italians that influence their grammar?"

AI Tools for Translators

Image credit: Google Translate

Google Translate supports over 100 languages and can handle text, voice, and even image-based translations.

DeepL is known for its high-quality translations and natural language output. It currently supports around 25 languages, but its translations are often considered more accurate and fluent than other AI translation tools.

Microsoft Translator provides translations for more than 70 languages and offers features such as real-time conversation translations and integration with Microsoft Office products.

Trados Studio offers AI-powered translation memory and terminology management, as well as a range of other features to help translators improve their productivity and maintain consistency across projects.

Phrase uses AI-powered translation memory, terminology management, and machine translation post-editing to help translators streamline their workflow and maintain translation quality.

Lilt.com is an AI-powered translation platform that combines machine translation with adaptive neural networks, allowing translators to train the system to improve translation quality over time based on their feedback and corrections.

Mate Translate (by gikken.co) offers instant translations for over 100 languages and features like text-to-speech and translation history.

Transcribers

A transcriber is a person or software that converts spoken language or audio recordings into written text, also known as a transcript. Transcribers are used in various fields, including legal, medical, business, and educational settings, where accurate documentation of spoken words is essential. The role of a transcriber may involve the following:

- Listening carefully to audio or video recordings and converting them into written text.
- Ensuring that the written text accurately reflects the content of the audio or video material, including the specific words, phrases, and expressions used by the speaker(s).
- Editing the transcript for readability and clarity while preserving the original meaning and context.
- Identifying and noting any unclear or inaudible parts of the recording.
- Formatting the transcript according to specific requirements, including timestamps, speaker identification, or adhering to a particular style guide.
- Proofreading and revising the transcript to ensure it is error-free and accurately represents the source material.

Using ChatGPT

ChatGPT can be a valuable tool for transcribers in several ways:

Automatic transcription: ChatGPT can generate an initial transcription of audio or video recordings, significantly reducing the time and effort required for manual transcription. Although the generated transcript may not be perfect, it can serve as a starting point for the transcriber to refine and edit.

Formatting assistance: ChatGPT can help transcribers format their transcripts according to specific guidelines or style requirements. The AI can be prompted to provide examples or guidance on formatting different transcript elements, such as speaker identification, timestamps, or section breaks.

Terminology clarification: If a transcriber encounters unfamiliar terms or jargon during the transcription process, ChatGPT can help provide explanations, definitions, or context, making it easier for the transcriber to understand and accurately transcribe the content.

Language support: ChatGPT can assist transcribers who work with content in multiple languages. The AI can provide translations, help with language-specific grammar or idiomatic expressions, and offer guidance on cultural nuances that may be important for accurate transcription.

Prompt Examples

- "Provide tips for maintaining accuracy and speed while transcribing audio recordings, including techniques for handling difficult accents, background noise, and unclear speech."
- "List the most effective tools and software for transcribers, such as transcription platforms, audio playback software, and noise-cancellation headphones."
- "Describe your approach to formatting and editing transcriptions, including your strategies for handling speaker identification, non-verbal cues, and time stamps."
- "Explain the process of converting a transcription into a subtitle or closed-caption file, and discuss the importance of timing, readability, and language adaptation for different American audiences."
- "Offer guidance on the following text to ensure idiomatic expressions are consistent with people living in Northern Canada: [Text]."

AI Tools for Transcribers

Otter.ai is a popular transcription service that uses AI to generate accurate transcriptions from audio and video files. In addition, it offers real-time transcription, speaker identification, keyword search, and collaboration features.

Trint.com combines AI-driven transcription with a user-friendly editor, allowing users to review and edit transcripts quickly. Moreover, it supports multiple languages and provides features such as speaker identification, timestamping, and export options.

Temi.com is an automated transcription service that uses advanced speech recognition technology to provide quick and affordable transcriptions. Also, the platform offers an easy-to-use editing interface and supports various export formats.

Sonix is an AI-powered transcription service that offers features like speaker identification, timestamps, and support for over 30 languages. It also provides an intuitive editor for reviewing and editing transcripts.

Rev.com is a transcription service offering both AI-generated and human-assisted transcriptions. Additionally, their AI-powered option, Rev.ai, provides fast and cost-effective automated transcription services.

Editors

An editor is a professional who works with written content to improve its clarity, coherence, accuracy, and overall quality. Editors play a crucial role in publishing, ensuring that the final output meets the desired standards and effectively communicates the intended message. An editor's specific tasks and responsibilities may vary depending on the type of content they work with and their specialization.

Successful editors should have strong language skills, attention to detail, critical thinking abilities, and excellent communication and collaboration skills. They should also be familiar with various style guides and be able to adapt to different types of content and subject matter. In general, editors perform the following tasks:

Review and evaluate content: Editors assess the quality, relevance, and suitability of written materials, such as articles, manuscripts, or reports, and determine if they meet the required standards for publication or distribution.

Edit and revise content: Editors correct grammar, spelling, punctuation, and syntax errors. They also improve sentence structure, coherence, and overall readability, ensuring that the text is clear, concise, and engaging.

Fact-checking: Editors verify the accuracy of the information presented in the content, cross-referencing sources and conducting research when necessary.

Style and format consistency: Editors ensure that the content adheres to the specific style guide or formatting guidelines, such as APA, MLA, or the organization's in-house style guide.

Provide feedback and guidance: Editors offer constructive feedback to writers, suggesting improvements and helping them refine their work. This often involves multiple rounds of revision and collaboration between the editor and the writer.

Content organization and structure: Editors may reorganize or restructure the content to improve its flow and ensure that it presents information logically and effectively.

Collaborate with other professionals: Editors often work closely with writers, designers, proofreaders, and other team members to ensure that the final output meets the desired quality and standards.

Editors may specialize in different areas, such as:

- Copy editing: Focuses on correcting grammar, spelling, punctuation, and syntax, as well as ensuring consistency and accuracy.
- Line editing: Involves a more in-depth examination of the text, improving sentence structure, clarity, and overall readability.
- Developmental editing: Addresses the broader aspects of the content, such as organization, structure, pacing, and coherence, to ensure that it effectively communicates the intended message.
- Proofreading: The final stage of editing involves checking for any remaining errors, inconsistencies, and formatting issues before publication.

Using ChatGPT

Here are some ways ChatGPT can help editors:

Rewriting and paraphrasing: ChatGPT can assist editors in rewriting or paraphrasing sentences or passages to improve clarity, readability, or conciseness while maintaining the original meaning.

Fact-checking: ChatGPT can be used to quickly verify basic facts or gather information on a topic, although it is essential to cross-reference the AI-generated answers with reliable sources to ensure accuracy.

Writer feedback: ChatGPT can help draft constructive feedback for writers, providing suggestions for improvement and helping editors communicate their thoughts effectively.

Content generation: ChatGPT can help generate ideas, outlines, or even complete drafts for articles or other written materials, which editors can then review, revise, and refine.

Content summaries: ChatGPT can assist in creating concise summaries of long texts or articles, which can benefit editors working with lengthy documents or manuscripts.

Research: ChatGPT can provide information on various topics, helping editors learn about a subject matter relevant to the content they are editing or stay up to date with industry trends and best practices.

Prompt Examples

- "List the top strategies for improving the clarity, coherence, and overall quality of a piece of writing, including techniques for revising sentence structure, organization, and word selection."
- "Discuss common mistakes that writers make in their manuscripts and how to address these issues during the editing process, such as addressing inconsistencies in the plot, character development, style, or tone."
- "Describe the different levels of editing, including developmental editing, copyediting, and proofreading, and describe the specific tasks and considerations involved in each stage of the editing process."
- "What is your approach to providing constructive feedback to writers, including tips for balancing praise with criticism and effectively communicating suggestions for improvement."
- "Review the following text for grammar, spelling, and punctuation errors: [Text]."

AI Tools for Editors

In addition to Grammarly, ProWritingAid, and Hemingway, here are some of the best AI tools for editors:

LanguageTool.org is an open-source grammar, spelling, and style checker that supports multiple languages. In addition, it offers suggestions for improving grammar and style, making it a versatile tool for editors in different languages.

Google Docs incorporates AI-powered features like grammar and spelling checks, autocorrect, and smart compose, which can help editors streamline their workflow and make real-time improvements to the text.

Writer.com is an AI-driven writing assistant that focuses on maintaining brand consistency and tone in your content. It can be customized to follow your brand guidelines and offers suggestions to help editors ensure the content aligns with the desired style and voice.

Spotlight: Writesonic

 **Writesonic**

Writeson

📝 **Writers**

🏬 Ecommerce stores

📢 Marketing teams

🐿 Entrepreneurs

Use the AI Writer
Google Docs) to
content to perfect

Paraphrasing Tool

See all feature

Image credit: Writesonic

Writesonic is an AI-powered writing assistant with a mission to empower everyone to write anything and publish anywhere.

Its tools simplify creating, editing, and publishing articles, blog posts, ads, landing pages, ecommerce product descriptions, social media posts, and many other content formats.

AI Tools

Writesonic allows you to write blog posts of up to 1500 words in just 20 seconds. All you need to do is provide a topic in just 4-5 words. It's a fully automated AI writing generator that creates articles with little need for editing.

Photosonic is a web-based tool that lets you create realistic or artistic images from any text description using a state-of-the-art text-to-image AI model. The model is based on latent diffusion, a process that gradually transforms a random noise image into a coherent picture that matches the text.

Discover my favorite online business and marketing apps: https://subscribepage.io/mike-reuben

8. MAKE MONEY ONLINE WITH SOFTWARE APPS

Software applications have revolutionized the way we live, work, and interact with one another, becoming an integral part of modern life. From its humble beginnings as simple lines of code, software has grown into a complex and powerful tool that has transformed various aspects of our lives.

Some of the most significant innovations brought about by software include instant global communication through email and social media platforms, advanced data analysis and visualization, the rise of artificial intelligence and machine learning, and the democratization of knowledge through search engines and digital libraries. These breakthroughs have not only reshaped industries and economies but have also fundamentally altered our understanding of the world and our place in it. Finally, software code and technology are responsible for producing game-changing apps and devices, including Windows, Nintendo, Facebook, iPhone, and ChatGPT.

Software Development

Software development involves designing, creating, testing, and maintaining software applications. This process uses programming languages, frameworks, and tools to write code that can be compiled and run on a computer or other electronic device.

Software development can encompass a wide range of activities, from creating simple desktop applications to developing complex software systems for large organizations.

The process typically involves several stages, including requirements gathering, design, implementation, testing, and maintenance.

The first stage of software development is requirements gathering, which involves identifying the needs and objectives of the software application. Once the requirements have been identified, the design stage begins, where the software architecture and user interface are planned out. The implementation then follows, which involves writing code and building the software.

After the implementation stage, the software is tested to ensure it works as expected and meets the requirements identified in the first stage. Any bugs or errors are identified and fixed before the software is released to users.

Once the software is released, maintenance and support become essential aspects of the software development process. This involves updating the software to fix bugs or add new features and providing technical support to users who encounter issues with the software.

Image credit: Pixabay

App Developers

An app developer designs, builds, tests, and maintains software applications for various platforms, such as mobile devices (iOS, Android), web browsers, or desktop computers. Their responsibilities encompass a wide range of tasks involving technical and creative skills.

Key Tasks

Conceptualizing: An app developer works with clients or team members to brainstorm and develop the concept for an application, identifying its purpose, target audience, and desired functionality.

Designing: They create the visual layout and user interface (UI) of the app, ensuring it is intuitive, user-friendly, and visually appealing. This may involve working with UI/UX designers or creating wireframes and mockups.

Coding: App developers write the code to bring the app's functionality to life, using programming languages like Swift or Objective-C for iOS, Java or Kotlin for Android, or JavaScript, HTML, and CSS for web apps.

Integrating: They integrate various components, such as databases, APIs, or third-party services, to enable the app's desired functionality and ensure seamless communication between different parts of the system.

Testing: App developers thoroughly test the application, identifying and fixing bugs, performance issues, or compatibility problems to ensure it works flawlessly across different devices, operating systems, and browsers.

Deployment: They deploy the app to app stores (such as Apple App Store or Google Play Store) or web servers, adhering to platform-specific guidelines and requirements.

Maintenance and updates: App developers monitor the app's performance, troubleshoot issues, and release updates to fix bugs, add new features, or improve user experience. They also ensure compatibility with new device models, operating systems, or software updates.

Documentation: They document their work, including the app's architecture, code, and functionality, which helps other developers understand the project and facilitates future updates or maintenance.

Getting Started

App developers can start their journeys by following steps that involve gaining the necessary skills, building a portfolio, and exploring job opportunities or freelance projects. Here is a guide to help aspiring app developers get started:

Choose a platform: Decide whether you want to develop iOS, Android, or web apps. This choice will determine the programming languages, tools, and resources you must learn.

Learn programming languages: Acquire knowledge of programming languages relevant to your chosen platform. For example, for iOS, learn Swift or Objective-C; for Android, learn Java or Kotlin; and for web development, learn HTML, CSS, and JavaScript.

Familiarize yourself with development tools: Learn how to use development environments and tools essential for your chosen platform. For example, for iOS, get acquainted with Xcode; for Android, learn Android Studio; and for web development, explore tools like Visual Studio Code, Sublime Text, or Atom.

Gain practical experience: Apply your knowledge by working on personal projects or contributing to open-source initiatives. In addition, building a few small apps from scratch will help you understand the development process and improve your skills.

Build a portfolio: Showcase your skills and projects through an online portfolio or GitHub repository. This will help potential clients or employers evaluate your expertise and experience.

Learn about app store guidelines: Familiarize yourself with the app submission and review process for your chosen platform and any procedures or requirements necessary for a successful launch.

Explore job opportunities or freelance work: Apply for entry-level positions, internships, or freelance projects to gain real-world experience and build a professional network. Then, as your skills and portfolio grow, you can pursue more advanced roles or even start your own app development business.

Many e-learning companies offer app development courses, including Coursera, edX, Codecademy, and Udemy.

Monetization

App developers can generate income through various channels, depending on their skills, preferences, and business models. Here are some common ways app developers make money:

Salary or hourly pay: Many app developers work as full-time or part-time employees for companies, startups, or development agencies, earning a salary or hourly wages for their work.

Freelance projects: Some developers prefer the flexibility of working as freelancers, taking on individual projects from clients and charging a fixed fee or hourly rate for their services.

Developing apps: Developers can create and launch applications on app stores like Apple's App Store or Google Play Store. They can earn money through the following:

- In-app purchases: Offering premium content, features, or virtual goods that users can buy within the app.
- Paid apps: Charging users a one-time fee to download and use the app.
- Subscriptions: Providing access to premium content or features regularly, such as monthly or yearly subscriptions.
- In-app advertising: Displaying ads within the app and earning revenue based on impressions, clicks, or user actions.

App reskinning: Developers can purchase app source codes, modify the design and features, and then launch the "reskinned" app as a new product. This can be a faster and more cost-effective way to launch an app, leveraging existing code and functionality.

Consulting or teaching: Experienced app developers can offer consulting services, help clients with app development strategies, or teach app development courses, workshops, or webinars.

Licensing software or technology: Developers with unique or innovative software solutions can license their technology to other companies or developers for a fee, generating passive income.

Affiliate marketing: Developers can earn commissions by promoting third-party products or services within their apps, driving users to make purchases or sign up for services.

Writing or content creation: Developers with solid writing skills can create content about app development, such as articles, e-books, or online courses, and earn money through sales, advertising, or affiliate marketing.

Using ChatGPT

Documentation: Developers can use ChatGPT to generate well-structured and clear documentation for their apps, including user guides, developer documentation, or API documentation, making it easier for others to understand and use their work.

Code explanations: ChatGPT can help developers understand complex code snippets or algorithms by providing plain language explanations, making learning new concepts or debugging issues easier.

Comment generation: Developers can use ChatGPT to generate meaningful comments for their code, improving readability and maintainability.

Error resolution: Developers can use ChatGPT to help troubleshoot and identify potential solutions for coding issues or bugs during the development process.

Content creation: Developers can use ChatGPT to generate engaging content for their app's marketing materials, blog posts, social media updates, or even in-app text, enhancing user experience and brand messaging.

Prompt Examples

Prompt to write a new code for a new feature or functionality:

- Act as a [Technology Name] developer
- [Write a detailed description]

Prompt with technology stack and other details:

- Act as: [Enter your profile]
- Technology stack: [Enter your technology stack]
- Functionality: [Enter functionality]
- Mandatory fields: [Enter Fields]
- Optional fields: [Enter Fields]
- Task: [Write a task description]

Prompt for fixing bugs and coding errors:

- Tell me how to debug the code to solve the given error.
- Project: [Project name/description]
- Technology stack: [Technology Stack]
- Error: [Explain the error]

Prompt for database tasks:

- Write a [Language] Query
- Tables: [Tables/collection list]
- Requirement: [Mention your requirement]

AI Tools for App Developers

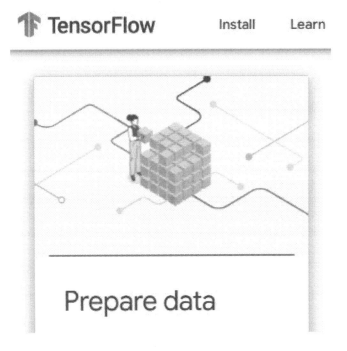

Image credit: TensorFlow

TensorFlow.org: Developed by Google, TensorFlow is a popular open-source machine learning library that helps developers build, train, and deploy machine learning models within their apps.

ML Kit: A Google-powered SDK that enables developers to integrate pre-built machine learning models for various functionalities like text recognition, face detection, and image labeling into their Android and iOS apps with ease.

Core ML: Apple's machine learning framework for iOS developers, allowing them to integrate machine learning models into their apps for tasks such as image recognition, natural language processing, and more.

IBM Watson: A suite of AI services and tools by IBM, which includes APIs for natural language understanding, visual recognition, and text-to-speech that developers can incorporate into their apps.

Microsoft Azure Cognitive Services: A collection of APIs and services from Microsoft that enable developers to add AI capabilities like speech recognition, computer vision, and language understanding to their apps.

Dialogflow: A Google-owned platform that enables developers to build conversational interfaces and chatbots for their apps, supporting text and voice interactions.

Hugging Face Transformers: A popular open-source library for natural language processing that provides pre-trained models and tools for tasks like text classification, summarization, and translation, which can be integrated into apps for enhanced language capabilities.

Amazon Lex: A service by AWS for building conversational interfaces using voice and text, allowing developers to create chatbots and voice assistants for their apps.

MonkeyLearn: A machine learning platform that helps developers with text analysis tasks, such as sentiment analysis, keyword extraction, and topic classification, which can be integrated into their apps using APIs.

App Designers

An app designer creates the visual elements, user interface (UI), and overall user experience (UX) of a software application. Their primary goal is to ensure that the app is visually appealing, intuitive, and easy to use.

App designers work closely with app developers, project managers, and other stakeholders to transform ideas and concepts into functional and engaging applications.

Key Tasks

Concept development: App designers collaborate with clients or team members to understand the app's objectives, target audience, and desired features, helping to shape the overall concept and vision of the application.

User research: They conduct user research, surveys, and interviews to gather insights about the target audience's needs, preferences, and pain points, which inform the app's design decisions.

Information architecture: App designers define the app's structure, organizing content and features in a logical and user-friendly manner. They create sitemaps, user flows, and navigation schemes to ensure a seamless user experience.

Wireframing and prototyping: They develop wireframes and prototypes to visualize the app's layout, user interface, and interactions. These mockups serve as blueprints for the developers and help stakeholders understand the app's functionality.

Visual design: App designers create the visual elements of the app, such as color schemes, typography, iconography, and imagery, ensuring that the outcome aligns with the app's branding and appeals to the target audience.

User Interface (UI) design: They design the app's user interface, including buttons, menus, and other interactive elements, adhering to platform-specific design guidelines and best practices, such as Apple's Human Interface Guidelines or Google's Material Design.

User Experience (UX) design: App designers focus on optimizing the app's overall user experience, ensuring that it is intuitive, enjoyable, and efficient. They incorporate user feedback and usability testing to identify and address potential issues or areas for improvement.

Design iteration and updates: Designers are responsible for refining and updating the app's design based on user feedback, analytics, or changing requirements. They continuously improve the app's usability and aesthetics to keep it relevant and engaging.

Image credit: Pixabay

Getting Started

Aspiring app designers can start their journeys by acquiring the necessary skills, building a portfolio, and exploring job opportunities or freelance projects. Get started in app design with these steps:

Learn the fundamentals—Acquire knowledge of design principles, color theory, typography, and visual hierarchy. Understanding these basics will help create visually appealing and functional designs.

Study UI/UX design principles—Learn the core principles of user interface (UI) and user experience (UX) design, which are essential for creating user-friendly and engaging applications.

Familiarize yourself with design tools—Learn how to use popular design tools and software, such as Sketch, Adobe XD, Figma, or InVision, which are widely used in the industry for creating wireframes, prototypes, and visual designs.

Understand platform-specific guidelines—Study platform-specific design guidelines, such as Apple's Human Interface Guidelines or Google's Material Design, to create designs that align with user expectations and best practices.

Gain practical experience—Apply your knowledge by working on personal projects, redesigning existing apps, or collaborating with others on real-world projects. This hands-on experience will help you understand the design process and improve your skills.

Build a portfolio—Showcase your skills and projects through an online portfolio, which will help potential clients or employers evaluate your expertise and experience. Include a variety of projects, highlighting your design process, problem-solving abilities, and creative thinking.

Learn about user research and testing—Understand the importance of user research and usability testing in the design process. Familiarize yourself with research methods like surveys, interviews, and user testing to gather insights and feedback that inform your design decisions.

Network with other designers—Join online forums and social media groups, or attend local meetups and conferences to connect with fellow designers, exchange ideas, and learn about new trends and technologies.

Explore job opportunities or freelance work—Apply for entry-level positions, internships, or freelance projects to gain real-world experience and build a professional network. Then, as your skills and portfolio grow, you can pursue more advanced roles or start your own design business.

Monetization

App designers make money in many of the same ways as app developers. However, the following ways are unique to app designers:

Partnering with developers: Designers can collaborate with app developers to create and launch apps, sharing the profits or revenue generated from the application.

Design templates or UI kits: App designers can create and sell design templates, UI kits, or other design resources to other designers or developers, generating passive income.

Stock assets: Designers can create and sell stock assets, such as icons, illustrations, or user interface components, on marketplaces like Adobe Stock, Shutterstock, or Dribbble.

Using ChatGPT

Design feedback: Designers can use ChatGPT to generate feedback on their designs, exploring potential issues or areas for improvement from a fresh perspective.

User research questions: ChatGPT can help designers develop user research questions, surveys, or interview scripts to gather valuable insights about their target audience's needs and preferences.

Design inspiration: Designers can use ChatGPT to find design inspiration by generating a list of apps or websites with similar features, aesthetics, or target audiences.

Content creation: Designers can use ChatGPT to create engaging content for their app's marketing materials, blog posts, social media updates, or even in-app text, enhancing user experience and brand messaging.

Design explanations: ChatGPT can provide plain language explanations of complex design concepts or guidelines, making it easier for designers to learn new principles or communicate their ideas to clients or team members.

Portfolio presentation: Designers can leverage ChatGPT to generate compelling descriptions or narratives for their portfolio projects, highlighting their design process, problem-solving abilities, and creative thinking.

Prompt Examples

- "Explain the design features of Apple's App Store icon."
- "Describe the process of creating user personas and their importance in the app design process, and share your approach to incorporating user feedback to refine and improve the app experience."
- "Discuss the principles of effective user interface (UI) and user experience (UX) design, and explain how you apply these principles to create intuitive, engaging, and visually appealing app designs."
- "Share your insights on designing app navigation and information architecture, including considerations for making the app's content easily accessible and discoverable while minimizing cognitive load for users."
- "Provide a textual description of a simple wireframe for a fashion app to help design the layout."

AI Tools for App Designers

Uizard is an AI-powered design tool that can convert hand-drawn sketches into digital wireframes or high-fidelity prototypes, simplifying the design process for app designers.

Framer.com is a design and prototyping tool incorporating AI-powered features, allowing designers to create responsive and interactive designs for various devices and screen sizes.

B12.io is a website builder that uses AI technology to generate custom designs based on user input, streamlining the design process and enabling designers to create responsive layouts quickly.

Loka by Logojoy is an AI-powered logo generator that helps designers create unique, professional-looking logos based on their preferences and branding guidelines.

Google AutoDraw is an AI-powered drawing tool that can recognize and correct hand-drawn sketches, providing designers with refined and professional-looking illustrations.

Wix ADI is a website builder that uses AI to create personalized web designs based on user preferences and input, which can save time in the initial design stages.

9. BOOST YOUR EMPLOYMENT PROSPECTS

AI has brought about significant changes to the way employees work and interact within the modern workplace. AI tools are transforming various aspects of work, enhancing efficiency, automating routine tasks, and enabling more intelligent decision-making. These powerful technologies have the potential to unlock new opportunities for employees, fostering collaboration, innovation, and productivity. However, alongside these benefits, AI also presents challenges, as workers must adapt to new ways of working and develop the skills needed to harness the potential of AI tools.

In this evolving landscape, understanding the impact of AI on employees is crucial for both individuals and organizations seeking to thrive in the future of work.

Employees

Are you a manager of a team at a large enterprise? Are you an executive assistant? Do you have to create presentations for colleagues? Are you responsible for content marketing at your company?

Although this book covers ways to make money online in the spirit of entrepreneurship, employees can benefit tremendously from using ChatGPT and other AI tools. It's only a matter of searching and experimenting with various apps to improve results.

Using ChatGPT

By using ChatGPT to support employees, organizations can improve employee satisfaction and retention, reduce HR costs, and enhance productivity, onboarding, training, and performance. First, however, it's vital to ensure that employees are comfortable using ChatGPT and that it is not used as a replacement for human interaction where needed.

Prompt Examples

- "Suggest ideas or activities to manage an underperforming manager."
- "List five free web meeting apps for online meetings, video conferencing, and collaboration."
- "Describe your approach to problem-solving and critical thinking in a work setting, including how you identify and analyze issues, generate potential solutions, and evaluate their feasibility and impact."
- "Discuss the importance of effective communication in the workplace, and provide tips for improving both verbal and written communication skills, such as active listening, asking questions, and using clear language."
- "Explain how to navigate workplace conflicts and maintain positive professional relationships, including strategies for addressing disagreements, handling difficult conversations, and finding common ground with colleagues."

AI Tools for Employees

AI tools have become essential for businesses to improve productivity, streamline processes, and enhance employee performance. Some of the best AI tools for employees include:

Communication and Collaboration Tools

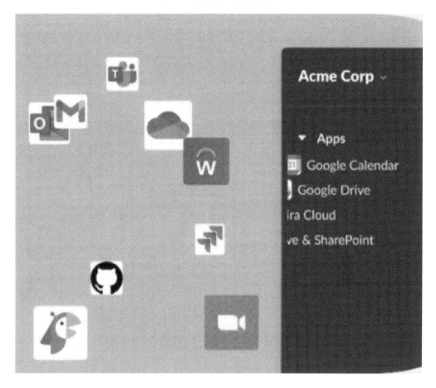

Image credit: Slack

- Slack: A team collaboration tool that uses AI for intelligent suggestions and streamlining workflows.
- Microsoft Teams: Offers AI-powered features such as meeting transcription, translation, and replies.

Project Management and Task Automation

- Asana: Helps teams track work with AI-powered project management and prioritization features.
- Trello: A visual project management tool that uses AI to suggest tasks, deadlines, and relevant team members.

Virtual Assistants and Chatbots

- Google Assistant: Provides voice and text-based assistance to help with scheduling, reminders, and email management.
- Chatbot: Simulates human-like conversations with users via chat.

Customer Relationship Management (CRM) Tools

- Salesforce Einstein: AI-powered CRM that provides predictive lead scoring, automated data entry, and intelligent recommendations.
- HubSpot: Offers AI-driven marketing, sales, and customer service tools that help employees work more efficiently.

Data Analytics and Business Intelligence Tools

- Tableau: A powerful data visualization tool incorporating AI for advanced data analysis and forecasting.
- Power BI: Microsoft's AI-driven analytics tool that helps employees create data-driven reports and gain insights.

Document Management and Collaboration

- Google Workspace: Offers AI-powered features like smart compose, grammar suggestions, and real-time collaboration in documents, sheets, and slides.

Those are just a few examples of the many AI tools available to help employees in various industries. Of course, the best AI tools for your organization will depend on your specific needs, goals, and the tasks your employees perform.

Recruiters

A recruiter finds, attracts, and hires qualified candidates for job vacancies in organizations. Recruiters can work in-house for a company or organization or for an external recruiting agency that provides recruiting services to multiple clients.

Recruiters typically work closely with hiring managers and human resources professionals to identify staffing needs, develop job descriptions, and create recruitment strategies. They may also use various recruiting tools and techniques, such as job boards, social media, networking events, and employee referrals, to identify potential candidates.

Once potential candidates are identified, recruiters may conduct initial screening interviews, review resumes and application materials, and conduct background checks and other assessments to ensure that candidates meet the job requirements. They may also negotiate job offers and facilitate the hiring process, including coordinating interviews and providing feedback to candidates.

Recruiters may specialize in a particular industry or function, such as technology, healthcare, or finance. They may also specialize in recruiting for types of positions, such as executive roles, entry-level jobs, or specialized technical functions.

In addition to finding and hiring candidates, recruiters may play a key role in employer branding and promoting the organization's culture and values to potential candidates. They may also provide guidance and support to candidates throughout the hiring process, including providing feedback, answering questions, and addressing any concerns or issues that may arise.

Getting Started

To get started as a recruiter, there are several steps you can take:

- Obtain the necessary education and training: While there is no specific degree or certification required to become a recruiter, a background in business, human resources, or a related field can be helpful. Many colleges and universities offer degree programs in these fields, and professional development courses and certifications are available through industry organizations.

- Gain experience: Many recruiters start their careers in entry-level roles in human resources or recruiting, such as an HR assistant or recruiter coordinator. This can provide valuable experience in recruiting processes, candidate screening, and interviewing techniques.
- Develop recruiting skills: Recruiters must be skilled in various areas, including candidate sourcing, interviewing, and negotiation. Many resources are available to help you develop these skills, including online courses, professional development programs, and industry conferences.
- Consider working for a recruiting agency: Many recruiters get their start working for a recruiting agency, which can provide valuable experience and exposure to various industries and job functions.

Image credit: LinkedIn

Making Money

Recruiters can make money in various ways, depending on their employment status and the nature of their work. Here are some of the most common ways that recruiters earn an income:

Salary: Many recruiters work as employees of a company or organization and receive a salary for their work. In this case, their compensation is not tied directly to the number of candidates they place or the fees generated by their work.

Commission: Some recruiters work on a commission basis, meaning they are paid a percentage of the salary of the candidate they place. Commission rates can vary widely depending on the industry, location, and type of position being filled. For example, a recruiter may earn a commission of 20-30% of the candidate's first-year salary.

Retainer: In some cases, recruiters may work on a retainer basis, meaning they are paid a flat fee for their services regardless of the number of candidates they place. Retainer fees are typically paid upfront or in installments throughout the recruitment process.

Contingency fee: A contingency fee is paid to a recruiter only if they successfully place a candidate in a job. The price is typically a percentage of the candidate's salary and is paid by the employer rather than the candidate.

Contract work: Some recruiters work as independent contractors and may be paid on an hourly or project basis. In this case, their compensation is tied directly to the amount of work they perform and the terms of their contract.

Using ChatGPT

ChatGPT can help recruiters in a variety of ways, including:

Candidate screening: ChatGPT can screen and pre-qualify candidates for job openings. Recruiters can create chatbots that use natural language processing to ask candidates questions about their qualifications, experience, and job preferences. This can help recruiters save time and focus their efforts on candidates who are the best match for the job.

Job matching: ChatGPT can also be used to match candidates with job openings based on their skills, experience, and preferences. Recruiters can use chatbots to ask candidates about their qualifications and job preferences and then match them with job openings that meet their criteria.

Scheduling interviews: ChatGPT can schedule interviews with candidates, freeing up recruiters' time for other tasks. Chatbots can be programmed to ask candidates about their availability and schedule interviews automatically based on the recruiter's calendar.

Answering candidate questions: ChatGPT can also be used to answer candidates' questions about job openings, application procedures, and other topics. Chatbots can be programmed to provide information about the company, the job requirements, and the hiring process, and they can also answer frequently asked questions.

Streamlining communication: ChatGPT can help recruiters communicate more efficiently with candidates and hiring managers. Chatbots can send automated messages and reminders to candidates and provide real-time updates on the status of job applications and interview scheduling.

Prompt Examples

- "Create a document that I can use to interview someone in our organization who is hiring for a new sales position."
- "Explain your approach to evaluating candidate qualifications, including reviewing resumes, conducting interviews, and assessing soft skills, technical skills, and cultural fit with the organization."
- "Share best practices for managing a positive candidate experience throughout the recruitment process, such as providing timely communication, offering constructive

feedback, and ensuring a transparent and respectful hiring process."

- "Describe how you build and maintain a diverse and inclusive talent pipeline, including strategies for attracting and retaining candidates from underrepresented backgrounds and fostering a culture of inclusion within the organization."
- "Act like a researcher. Then, give me a list of keywords to use in a job description for a summer intern at a PR agency."

AI Tools for Recruiters

LinkedIn's Talent Insights platform uses AI to provide recruiters valuable data-driven insights about talent pools, competitive intelligence, and market trends. This helps recruiters make more informed decisions about their hiring strategies.

HireVue is an AI-powered video interviewing platform that uses machine learning algorithms to assess candidates' verbal and non-verbal cues, helping recruiters identify the best candidates quickly and efficiently.

Textio is an AI-driven writing platform that helps recruiters create more inclusive and effective job descriptions. It analyzes language patterns and suggests improvements to attract a diverse pool of qualified candidates.

Pymetrics uses neuroscience games and AI to assess candidates' cognitive and emotional traits, providing recruiters with valuable insights to make better hiring decisions. This ensures a more objective and data-driven approach to candidate selection.

Eightfold.ai is an AI-powered talent intelligence platform that helps recruiters manage the entire hiring process, from candidate sourcing and engagement to interview scheduling and evaluation. Its deep learning algorithms analyze candidates' skills, experiences, and potential to match them with the right job opportunities.

171

XOR is an AI recruitment chatbot that automates communication with candidates, providing instant answers to their questions and helping recruiters save time on routine tasks. XOR can also pre-screen candidates, schedule interviews, and send reminders.

Ideal.com is an AI-powered talent screening and matching tool that helps recruiters automate the candidate sourcing and screening process. It uses machine learning algorithms to analyze resumes, social profiles, and other data points, enabling recruiters to identify top talent quickly.

Fetcher.ai is an AI-driven sourcing platform that automates finding and engaging with potential candidates. It uses machine learning algorithms to identify the best-fit candidates based on their skills, experiences, and other factors.

Harver.com is a pre-employment assessment platform that uses AI to evaluate candidates' skills and cultural fit. It offers a range of customizable assessments, including situational judgment tests, cognitive ability tests, and work samples.

10. YOUR CHATGPT AND AI JOURNEY START NOW

The use of AI tools such as ChatGPT has revolutionized how we make money online. With its ability to understand human language and generate human-like responses, ChatGPT has made it possible for businesses to automate customer service, generate leads, and increase conversions. Other AI tools, such as predictive analytics, natural language processing, and machine learning algorithms, have also made it easier for businesses to optimize their online presence and make data-driven decisions.

As we move towards an increasingly digital world, the role of AI in making money online will only continue to grow. While there are still challenges to overcome, such as ensuring the ethical use of AI and addressing concerns around job displacement, the benefits of AI in driving economic growth and improving customer experience are undeniable.

Whether you're an entrepreneur looking to start a new business, a marketer seeking to optimize your online presence, or an investor looking for new opportunities, understanding how to leverage AI tools like ChatGPT is crucial for success in today's digital economy. With the right strategies and tools in place, the possibilities for making money online using AI are virtually limitless.

All the best in making money online, leveling up your business, and using AI tools.

Sincerely,

Mike Reuben

Please leave a review to support others like you, this book, and my future book releases. Many thanks for considering my big request.

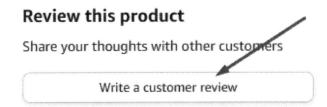

Review this product

Share your thoughts with other customers

Write a customer review

Discover my favorite online business and marketing apps: https://subscribepage.io/mike-reuben